11 Jan 19

C000200324

# How to Get a
# You Love

# How to Get a Job You Love

## 2019–20 Edition

**John Lees**

 Open University Press

How to Get a Job You Love
2019–20 Edition
John Lees

ISBN: 9781526847140
e-ISBN: 9781526847157

Published by McGraw-Hill Education
8th Floor, 338 Euston Road
London
NW1 3BH
UK

Telephone: +44(0) 20 3429 3400
Website: www.mheducation.co.uk

British Library Cataloguing in Publication Data
A catalogue record for this book is available from the British Library

Library of Congress Cataloguing in Publication Data
The Library of Congress data for this book
is available from the Library of Congress

Publishing Director: Teresa Massara
Commissioning Editor: Hannah Kenner
Editorial Assistant: Karen Harris
Content Product Manager: Ali Davis

Typeset by Transforma Pvt. Ltd., Chennai, India

McGraw-Hill Education books are available at special quantity
discounts to use as premiums and sales promotions or for use in
corporate training programs. To contact a representative, please
email b2b@mheducation.com

# PRAISE FOR *HOW TO GET A JOB YOU LOVE*

'A positive, practical and readable guide, packed with creative tools and common sense advice from an author who understands careers from all angles. This book will support and encourage you throughout your working life, from making your initial career decision to helping with long term career management. It will challenge your preconceptions of yourself and of the world of work, and help you to a more fulfilling career.'

**Julia Yates, Programme Director,**
**MSc Organisational Psychology,**
**City, University of London**

'This is THE definitive careers book which just keeps on getting better. I recommend it to listeners on my podcast and to my coaching clients, as it is up to date and provides clear, accessible and engaging career guidance which will help readers no matter what stage they are in their job seeking journey. Life is too short to spend your time doing a job you don't enjoy. This book gives you the practical step-by-step skills, exercises and strategies you will need to get the job you'll love.'

**James Curran, Career**
**coach and podcast host at**
**www.graduatejobpodcast.com**

'An absolute cracker of a book that will quite literally change your life as well as your career. I am always excited to explore the latest ideas presented in this essential career book every time it is revised, and am always inspired by what I find. Wherever you are on your own career path, simply buy this book – and have John by your side as you navigate your way to a place you didn't think was possible.'

**Kathryn Jackson, New Zealand Leadership Coach and author of *Resilience at Work***

'I love the way that this book evolves; and it's important that John has set this edition in the context of the changing nature of organisations and careers. Most of us will no longer be in a job for life. Many will find their values and life goals change, and so we need to review and consider what's best for us right now. Inside this book are many helpful activities to get you thinking and moving to a more satisfying option.'

**Denise Taylor, Career Psychologist with Amazing People and author of *Find Work at 50+***

'I frequently recommend job seekers or those at a career crossroads to read *How to Get a Job You Love* as it offers practical and easily accessible advice from someone with vast experience in the area.'

**Joëlle Warren MBE, DL, Executive Chair, Warren Partner*s***

'For years, John Lees has been the smartest voice in career coaching. His insight and advice are a must-read for anyone entering today's competitive job market.'

**Rebecca Alexander, Dossier Editor, *Psychologies Magazine***

'Thank you John, for producing yet another *How to Get a Job You Love* masterpiece, now in its 10th edition. This latest edition combines John's extensive wisdom of the complex world of careers, with heaps of practical and accessible advice on enhancing your career prospects. With new features such as up to the minute advice on using social media in your job search, and fine-tuning your "career narrative", this is a "must-read" for anyone who wants to maximise their job satisfaction and explore the next step in their career.'

**Sophie Rowan, bestselling author of *Brilliant Career Coach – How to Find and Follow your Dream Career***

'Watch out – this book could turn your life upside down.'

**Liz Hall, Editor, *Coaching At Work***

'John is a regular speaker at AMBA events. His highly practical approach and engaging style of career coaching made him the obvious choice to launch and continue to contribute to AMBA's webinar series. Alongside the various editions of *How To Get A Job You Love* and his other titles, business schools repeatedly welcome John to dispense real-world advice to MBA students and alumni. In my own coaching practice John's techniques are enthusiastically actioned by clients as they design (and achieve) their next role either as an in-house promotion or elsewhere.'

**Steve Gorton, Enabling Development; Trustee Director – Association of MBAs (2008–2015***)*

'This practical guide is a well-thumbed book in our school Careers Library. John Lees' advice and guidance is as useful to young people as it is to adults.'

**James Brittain, Head of Careers and Higher Education, Millfield School**

'The popularity of John Lees' writing lies in his ability to connect with the sense many people have that they can be more than they currently are and deserve greater job satisfaction than they currently have. What makes his work distinctive is his use of his wide experience in careers coaching to provide tools and ways of thinking that any motivated individual can easily use to take control of their working life.'

**Carole Pemberton, Career and Executive Coach and author of *Coaching to Solutions***

'John Lees advice on careers is always useful and interesting and often surprising and even fascinating. From getting ahead to changing your career completely, this book is great guide to navigating the treacherous waters of the modern workplace.'

**Rhymer Rigby, FT journalist and author of *28 Business Thinkers Who Changed The World***

'I know first hand the joy that being in the right career can bring and I commend John Lees for his books and seminars which help other people do just that.'

**Rosemary Conley CBE**

This book, like all previous editions,
is dedicated to someone
who has been special to me
for a very long time.

To my wife, Jan,
for giving me space to find out.

# Contents

# List of exercises

# Foreword – in memory of Richard Nelson Bolles

*(Dick Bolles wrote this foreword for an earlier edition of the book, before his sad death in March 2017. This text is reprinted with the permission of Dick's estate.)*

You would not believe how many career and job-hunting books cross my path each year. New ones appear at my door week by week. All of them have some good ideas, of course, but only a few really stand out. John Lees' classic work is one of those. I cannot recommend it highly enough. It is thorough, inventive, truth-telling and helpful. I have known John, and this book, for a long, long time. John was a student of mine, twice in fact, back when dinosaurs were still roaming the earth. He was already well known for his distinguished career, but since then he has, as we say, gone from strength to strength. We have stayed in touch all these years, in spite of the fact that I live across the pond (in the San Francisco Bay area, to be exact).

He is one of those people in life who is thoroughly worth staying in touch with. His integrity is rock-solid, he is always anxious to help as many people as possible, he is thoroughly grounded in a faith that means something, and he is an expert in his field. You want a book from such a man, you *hope for* a book from such a man. And, thank the good Lord, here it is.

Now used by countless numbers of people, who found themselves helped by the wisdom in these pages, this book is a treasure. Read it, devour it, use it, and find that job you once dreamed about but had almost given up on. Time to revive your dreams. This book will give you chariots to ride.

**Richard Nelson Bolles (1927–2017)**
Author of *What Color Is Your Parachute?*
*A Practical Manual for Job-Hunters*
*and Career-Changers*

# About the author

John Lees is one of the UK's best-known career strategists and the author of a wide range of business titles. *How to Get a Job You Love* regularly tops the list as the bestselling career change handbook by a British author and was twice selected as the WHSmith Business Book of the Month. John is the author of a wide range of career and business titles. His books have been translated into Arabic, Georgian, Polish, Japanese and Spanish. In 2012, he wrote the introduction to the *Harvard Business Review Guide to Getting the Right Job*.

John has written careers columns for *Metro* and *People Management*. He appears frequently in the national press and his work has been profiled in *Management Today, Psychologies, Coaching at Work* and *The Sunday Times*. TV appearances include the BBC interactive *Back to Work* series, BBC2's *Working Lunch,* Channel 4's *Dispatches*, ITV's *Tonight – How To Get A Job* and Sky News. He has delivered career workshops in Australia, Germany, Ireland, New Zealand, Mauritius, Spain, South Africa, Switzerland and several parts of the USA.

John is a graduate of the universities of Cambridge, London and Liverpool, and has spent most of his career focusing on the world of work, spending 25 years training recruitment specialists. He is the former Chief Executive of the Institute of Employment Consultants (now the Institute of Recruitment Professionals, IRP) and an Honorary Fellow of the IRP.

He has consulted for a wide range of organisations, including: British Gas Commercial, the British Council, CIPD, Endsleigh, Gumtree, Harrods, Hiscox, the House of Commons, ICAEW, Imperial College, the Association of MBAs, Lloyds Banking Group, Marks & Spencer, the National Audit Office, Standard Life, Totaljobs, as well as business schools across the UK. He served as Joint Chair of the Association of Career Professionals-UK (2011–13), was a founding Board Director of the Career Development Institute and, in March 2016, was elected a NICEC Fellow.

Alongside his day job, John serves as an ordained Anglican priest in the Diocese of Exeter and is the Bishop's Officer for Self-Supporting Ministry. John is married to the poet and children's writer Jan Dean.

John Lees Associates helps career changers in the UK and elsewhere. We specialise in helping people to make difficult career decisions – difficult either because they don't know what to do next or because there are barriers in the way of success.

w: www.johnleescareers.com
tw: @JohnLeesCareers
Facebook: www.facebook.com/JohnLeesCareers
LinkedIn: How To Get A Job You'll Love Network

# Acknowledgements

With age comes, perhaps later than it should, a realisation of those many people I haven't thanked enough.

I start by thanking Dick Bolles, author of the world-famous *What Color Is Your Parachute?* My work as a career strategist was inspired by the creativity, wisdom and generosity of 125 hours' teaching from Dick at two of his summer workshops in Bend, Oregon, followed by two decades of support and inspiration. His death in 2017 left a huge gap in the careers field.

I'm also grateful to those who have let me road-test ideas with different audiences: Mel Barclay (LHH Penna), Samantha Brown (ICAEW), Fabian Caton (Totaljobs), Janice Chalmers (Surrey University Business School), James Curran (Graduate Job Podcast), Helen Collins (Careers Springboard Bracknell), Lindsay Comalie (Imperial College), Jan Ellis (Career Development Institute), Fiona Hayes (AHECS, Ireland), Yasmina Mallam Hassam (Imperial College Business School), Marcia Hoynes and Wendy Pearson (Durham University Business School), Sarah Jackson (Warwick Business School), Becky Kilsby (Exeter University Business School), Rob Nathan (CCS), Kathryn Tolley (AMBA), Nicky Trainor (Organisation Development Institute, NZ), Pauline Watkins (RCA), Laura Woodward (Royal Society of Chemistry) and Marie Zimenoff (Career Thought Leaders).

My appreciation goes out to everyone who has asked great questions or shared brilliant ideas which have worked their way into this edition: Gill Best, Jo Bond, Marie Brett, Jim Bright, Julian Childs, Hilary Dawson, Sara Dewar, Zena Everett, Matthias Feist, Peter Fennah, Gill Frigerio, Wendy Hirsh, Ajaz Hussain, Kate Howlett, Kathryn Jackson, Esi Kpeglo, Stuart Lindenfield, Stuart McIntosh, Rosemary McLean, Adi Mechen, James Parsons, Bernard Pearce, Carole Pemberton, Rhymer Rigby, Valerie Rowles, Denise Taylor, Joëlle Warren and Ruth Winden. I'm enormously grateful to clients who have kindly agreed to be case studies in this book: Will Beale, Melissa Carr, Beth Grant, Simon Ryan, James Voûte and Mary Wilson.

My special thanks go to several people. To Kate Howlett, Managing Consultant at John Lees Associates, for all her encouragement and for many improvements to the manuscript. To Gill Best for partnering me on our Career Coach Masterclasses for many years. To Trevor Gilbert for being a great business mentor earlier in my career. To my brother Andrew Lees for his insights into thinking styles. To Jane Bartlett and Stuart Mitchell for reviewing the first edition, and to its commissioning editor at McGraw-Hill, Elizabeth Choules. Thanks also to my editor Hannah Kenner and the whole team at McGraw-Hill, especially Karen Harris and Ali Davis. I'd like to express enormous gratitude to Becky Charman for so efficiently managing my PR for many years, and to my agent James Wills at Watson, Little for his unstinting support. Finally, with sadness, my thanks go to my friend and talented publicist Sue Blake (1961–2012), without whom it wouldn't have been half as much fun.

**Other careers books by John Lees
published by McGraw-Hill Professional**

*Knockout Interview* **(2017),
ISBN 978-0077189563**
A definitive overview of the job interview process and how to prepare for it. Includes a wide range of example questions you will face, and strategies for how to answer them.

*Knockout CV* **(2013), ISBN 978-0077152857**
Building on an extensive review of what employers love and hate about CVs, helps you decide which CV format will work best for you. How to write CVs and cover letters that convey your strengths quickly and get you into the interview room.

*Career Reboot: 24 Tips for Tough Times* **(2009),
ISBN 978-0077127589**
Packed with quick-read, practical tips for rejuvenating your job search, this book is a must for anyone striking out into a difficult job market after redundancy or simply looking for new opportunities in a difficult market.

*Take Control of Your Career* **(2006),
ISBN 978-0077109677**
How to manage your career once you've got a job, learning how to read your organisation, avoid career traps, renegotiate your job role and enhance your future without losing control of your life balance.

# How to use this book

## Who is this book for?

This book is written for anyone who is trying to make informed decisions about career choice. This book can help you if you are:

- feeling 'stuck' and looking for new challenges, and wondering 'what on earth can I do?'
- ready to plan the next stage of your career
- facing redundancy, and asking 'what do I do next?'
- leaving full-time education or seeking work after bringing up a family
- unemployed and looking for better ways of identifying opportunities
- seeking work and short of ideas about job possibilities
- discouraged because you believe you have little to offer the labour market
- exploring the idea of finding a completely new career.

## How this book might help you

There are many 'how to' books about career change and job search. If you're looking for boxes to tick, 'to do' checklists, model CVs or letters, look at one of the hundreds of books available that will give you an organised, left-brain solution to career management. We all need good advice when it comes to managing our job search. These books work well if you have a clear sense of direction, and all you need is a more effective job search technique. However, they don't appear to help answer the most common career statement: 'I know I want to do something different, but I don't know what it is.' And just as important, the question: 'How do I take the first step towards making a change?'

The chapters ahead do something different. In these pages you will look at the way businesses and individuals generate ideas about products, services and organisations, and apply that creative energy to career planning. It will challenge your perceived limitations and help you to discover your strengths.

This book aims to unlock your hidden potential and apply it to your career and life planning, to make the way you spend your waking hours more creative, more meaningful, more enjoyable. Its focus is not on job change for its own sake. Quite simply, the aim is to help you to make connections between your natural creativity and the way you plan your life's work. As a result of reading it, you may discover tools to improve your present job and create career opportunities where you are now. Alternatively, you will find practical advice about making your chosen future happen.

You may find that a single exercise unlocks your potential, or you may gain multiple insights from using several ideas or exercises. One word of advice: if the exercise doesn't work for you, don't feel you have 'failed'. All it means is this: *the exercise doesn't work for you.* Put it aside and move on.

## Maps for the journey ahead

Chapter 1 helps put this book in the context of the way we think about work and careers in the twenty-first century, asking important questions about balancing work satisfaction against job market reality. Chapter 2 takes a hard look at what gets in the way, including psychological barriers to change. Chapters 3 and 4 invite you to take control of your career by thinking of it as a positive 'deal' between your personal drivers and what the market has to offer. Chapter 5 kick-starts your thinking about new career ideas by **showing you how to tap into new kinds of thinking.**

Chapters 6–9 offer you the chance to understand yourself better by exploring your **career hot buttons,** your hidden and motivated **skills,** your chosen areas of **knowledge,** and the key aspects of **personality** that will shape your career, including an overview of your **values.**

Once you have completed this central section of the book, you will be ready to complete your **Master Sheet** (see below).

If you're thinking about changing career path, look at Chapters 10 and 11, including the **Field Generator** – a ground-breaking tool to generate potential work sectors. Check out Chapter 12 on the range of working models you might consider, including a portfolio career.

Next, in Chapter 13, some highly practical advice on **smarter job searching.** Chapters 14 shows you how to connect **online** and manage your social media, and Chapter 15 encourages you to begin networking, and shows you how to conduct information interviews. Chapter 16 helps you sharpen up your **interview technique.**

Chapter 17 is written specially for those **moving into work after leaving full-time education**, including school leavers.

Appendix 1 is the **Master Sheet**, an opportunity for you to set out the results of key exercises on one page. Further on, Appendix 2 contains **CV and cover letter tips**, with examples. Appendix 3 outlines a range of **case studies** – people who have changed their careers using this book.

## Guest contributors

In this book, you will find not only my own views but advice from a wide range of experts:

- Peter Fennah on assessment events (Chapter 9)
- Joëlle Warren on working with executive recruiters (Chapter 13)
- Julian Childs, Matthias Feist and Ruth Winden on getting the best out of the internet and social media (Chapter 14)
- Kate Howlett on interview tips (Chapter 16)
- Denise Taylor on entering the job market for the first time (Chapter 17).

## New in this edition

This edition sees one of the biggest revisions and updates in the book's history. It contains up-to-date research and insights into the jobs market, a strategy for career success at a time of job fragility, and deeper insights into the ever-puzzling 'hidden' job market. The book continues to provide support for everyone asking the question, 'what kind of career would suit me best?'

New features in this edition include:

- What's going on in the current job market – continuing job fragility, insecurity.
- Updated material on managing your social media presence and impact.
- Effective job search strategies as more and more jobs are not advertised.
- Updated material on what will shorten (or extend) your job search.
- New material on creating a better career 'deal'.

- A completely revised chapter on job interviews, including material on competency-based interviews and telling your career story.
- New material on networking and reaching out using information interviews.
- New or largely revised exercises:
  - ○ Chapter 1: Breaking out of default mode
  - ○ Chapter 6: The 3-minute motivation checklist
  - ○ Chapter 9: Values exercises
  - ○ Chapter 10: From subjects of interest to occupational sectors; and Going deeper into sectors
  - ○ Chapter 12: Should I work for myself?

# 'Get a job you love?'
# Get real . . .

'There is no point in work unless it absorbs you like
an absorbing game.' **D.H. Lawrence**

*This chapter helps you to:*

- Gain insights into today's job market
- Understand how job hunting has changed dramatically
- Think about job fragility and career flexibility
- Rethink your career strategy, and start to take control for yourself.

## Earning a living

This chapter provides an overview of what work is about in the second decade of the twenty-first century, and whether we can hope to be happy in it.

I have occasionally had the interesting experience of standing next to someone picking up this book and reading its title out to a friend. I'm always interested to hear the reply. It will be anything from 'sounds interesting' to a cynical 'hmmm'.

Publishing a book titled *How to Get a Job You Love* every 24 months for two decades has required more than a little nerve in terms of the ups and downs of the job market. The first major jolt was the economic turbulence experienced after the last quarter of 2008, leading to what some called the 'great recession'. Just as we were emerging from those troubled times, and probably as a direct result of them, we hit a period of even greater uncertainty following the 2016 Brexit referendum. Many businesses across Europe find it hard to predict what trading conditions will be like in just two years' time.

The economy seems contradictory: we have skill short-ages and low levels of unemployment, yet at the same time many workers are in low-paid and insecure work. We have companies riding high on the back of buoyant stock markets, and yet 2018 also saw a range of high-visibility failures. Much of the UK was shaken by the collapse of Carillion – a huge organisation, connected into almost every part of society. In the spring, both Maplin and Toys R Us went into administration. Other dramas will no doubt unfold, and more workers will be seeking new career paths. Where does this volatility leave organisations trying to manage talent – and individuals managing their careers?

How can organisations plan for their future workforce needs when they have no idea what kind of business they will be in 12 months' time? Many still promise they will retain their best people, but such promises are easily put aside. In fairness, it's easy to see why. Organisations are having to reinvent themselves on the hoof, and nearly all planning has become short term. Organisations still need to attract talent, but market forces mean they have to rethink the idea of long-term retention and staff development. How will our best organisations continue to maintain standards in terms of engagement, diversity, and talent management? Some organisations will continue to shine; others will strug-gle to fulfil their employer branding promises.

What's needed, it seems, is a new deal, perhaps one that is more open and honest about the future of work. Organisa-tions that in the past offered career pathways will increasingly provide something valuable, but much more transitory; long-term staff retention may come to seem like an antiquated idea. Employers can after all offer a great deal – useful experience, intensive skill development, and the chance to work with exciting people, brands or technology. However, most are unable – credibly – to offer long-term career stability.

## Job hunting – a new game

Something interesting has happened in the world of work. Looking back over 10 editions of this book, it's interesting to see how job hunting has changed so dramatically. Until the early part of this century, jobs were much more visible. Many of them were advertised – obvious targets for job seekers, involving a relatively straightforward application process.

The great recession deepened a trend that was already happening. Jobs have gone under the radar. Fewer and fewer are advertised conventionally. Employers have learned many cheap and smart ways of attracting talent. Sometimes this is high-tech (for example, using social media, or attracting and enlisting crowds of would-be workers to websites). Others use a canny mix of social media, organisational job boards, and word of mouth. In today's marketplace, jobs are increasingly filled by low-cost, low-visibility, informal methods. What this means is significant growth in the hidden job market (see Chapter 13).

### Finding a job – the new skill set

Looking for a job effectively and quickly relies less on internet searching and form-filling, and more on conversations and connections – highly developed soft skills. If this seems outside your capability, don't despair. This book outlines the easiest ways of doing this, short cuts, and work-arounds for those who really dislike networking.

When most jobs were visible, even relatively passive job seekers usually found something, sometimes just as a result of bulk applications. Now, however, if you judge the state of the jobs market by the number of advertised positions available, you'll feel rather despondent. Compared with just ten years ago, individuals have far more responsibility to make things happen.

Many smart people tell me that job hunting looks to them like a rather dull, low-skill activity. Surely writing a CV isn't rocket science, and applying for jobs is just about filling in online forms and pressing 'send' . . .? If only. The reality is rather different. Today, looking for a new role, particularly if it's a senior job, a creative job, or a job in a niche or new sector, requires sophisticated skills – influencing, communicating, savvy use of social media, and the ability to build relationships quickly.

Some market entrants believe that looking for a job is rather like opening a new account with an online retailer – entering data onto screens. I'd like to suggest that the process is in fact more like trying to get elected to public office. You need a clear message, and you need to know how to get it across. You need to influence key decision-makers and to recruit supporters, ambassadors, champions, and mentors. Most of all, you need to learn how to be visible so that *jobs find you.*

### Job fragility

Employment levels in the UK were at an all-time high in early 2018, but the market will continue to experience 'churn' – rapid and sometimes unpredictable changes to workforce numbers, with companies swinging rapidly from cutbacks to new hiring programmes. Skill shortages will inevitably give candidates in some markets leverage, but others will inevitably face deeper insecurity, largely because they will have to spend more time during an average career applying for their own jobs in restructured organisations or looking outside for alternative employment.

Job insecurity shows no sign of diminishing. It will no doubt be magnified by cuts in the public sector, and other organisations reinventing themselves several times a decade. On the ground what this often means is time-limited contracts for senior roles, more interim appointments to avoid adding to the headcount, and zero-hours contracts for many positions. The last element has apparently had a big effect on the way younger people experience work. The Resolution Foundation outlined in its February 2018 report *The Kids Aren't Alright: A new approach to tackle the challenges faced by young people in the UK labour market* (www.resolutionfoundation.org) that because of the 'rise of atypical, insecure, work, a greater share of younger people are working in lower paying sectors . . . fewer younger workers are moving jobs, and moving up the career ladder, than previous generations. It will be years before we can fully understand how deep the labour market scars are from millennials spending long periods in insecure and low paid work.'

Workers of all ages express concerns about job security. This sense of job fragility is reinforced by the way that organisations reshape themselves repeatedly. Where organisations have restructured extensively, the psychological contract has clearly been weakened, if not torn up. This is most evident where staff have to apply for their own jobs, or have to perform work normally done by two people. Research published in 2016 by Professor Karina Nielsen of Norwich Business School revealed that when organisations restructure, there is a measurably negative effect on employee well-being – even where there are no job losses.

We all know someone who has been required to accept new working terms, and we all know someone who has been made redundant in the last five years. Widespread redundancies have a positive side: employers see many candidates who have been 'let go' in the past, so the stigma of redundancy has largely disappeared (unless you make an issue of the topic, as discussed later). Some parts of the working population have taken a real hit, particularly 16–24-year-olds, but the market has been tough on workers over fifty too, where underemployment can be as big a problem as unemployment.

## How work is changing

Zero-hours contracts have been mentioned above. At the beginning of 2018, over 900,000 people were working this way. These contracts allow employers to avoid making any commitments about the availability of work. Employers can send someone home with no notice. Critics of the practice say these contracts undermine job security and engagement, but others say that the system offers welcome flexibility, allowing organisations to create new jobs and offer hours that some find helpful or convenient.

If work is no longer a fixed part of your week, you'll naturally feel less secure, and be less committed to it. Most zero-hours workers would like to work more hours. Other interesting spin-off effects are that workers are often sent home when work pressure slackens off. This means that they sometimes only experience work when it's very busy, and don't have quieter times to think about how they could do the job better or improve systems, or time spent getting to know work colleagues. If you work only when the heat is on, the job becomes less rounded, with less opportunities to observe and learn from others.

Some in today's job market have found that the quality of jobs on offer has diminished – jobs are available, but they are sometimes poorly paid or offer only limited prospects for skill development or advancement. More than a few people in the economy have had to take on more than one job just to keep their heads above water, particularly where there is no guarantee of working hours in their main role.

## Seeing a bigger picture

Every job market has its paradoxes. It's also important to distinguish between what has actually happened and the way we feel about it. Statistics suggest that during the recent recession, there were up to six unemployed people chasing each vacancy. Yet during the same downturn many employers complained of skill shortages (the February 2018 edition of the Chartered Institute of Personnel and Development's *Labour Market Outlook* recorded the concerns of many employers about future problems filling roles with a smaller pool of EU nationals available).

Some sectors bucked the trend and have experienced continuous growth throughout the past decade. Newspaper headlines continue to enjoy bad news, but the UK boasts employment levels envied by most of its European neighbours. According to the Office for National Statistics (ONS) report *UK Labour Market: March 2018* (www.ons.gov), a record-breaking 32.2 million people were in work in the UK in January 2018. Between December 2017 and February 2018, a total of 816,000 job vacancies were recorded – 56,000 higher than a year earlier. These vacancies were not necessarily for full-time or permanent jobs. In its report *Recruitment Industry Trends 2016/17*, the Recruitment & Employment Confederation reported that the turnover of the UK's recruitment industry increased to £32.2 billion by 2017 – with nearly a million people placed in permanent roles, and 1.3 million temporary workers.

We are not yet in a seller's market where candidates can play job offers against each other. However, according to the ONS, in any three-month period around 650,000 UK workers change jobs – that's in addition to people entering work for the first time. Sometimes job mobility is forced on workers; at other times it seems an attractive option. One reflection of job confidence is the number of staff who choose to resign from one job in order to take up another. This interesting measure is what Financial Times journalist Sarah O'Connor calls the 'take this job and shove it' index. In January 2018, Marketing Week suggested in that four out of ten marketeers in the UK planned to leave their current role in the next three years. In December 2017, the Daily Mail reported that two-thirds of UK workers planned to change career, adding that most had 'not received a pay rise or promotion in the past year'. The last point is an important one. Pay increases in the last decade have not generally kept up with inflation; daily rates for contractors have declined in some sectors. Flatter and leaner organisations offer less opportunities for promotion. The feeling that you may not get a better job by moving elsewhere is one of the reasons people don't seek to change jobs unless forced to do so.

## New conditions, new thinking

A tight market has been positive for some people. Some people are saying, 'if I'm going to lose my job, I might as well find something interesting'. Naturally, a number of people have been saying, 'I just need any kind of job' – but this often reflects a low point in their job search cycle; they quickly discover that this undifferentiated message makes them singularly unattractive to employers.

What's happening inside organisations is in some ways a good indicator of how we should operate when trying to get into them. Organisations have become leaner, with fewer rungs on the ladder and therefore fewer options for promotion. Individuals often have to make lateral moves to new divisions or teams in order to advance, often relying heavily on inside information plus support from both champions and mentors. These pathways are certainly not textbook, and not clear when you join an organisation. Lateral moves require lateral thinking, and your employer probably won't do it for you.

Significant numbers also consider alternatives to conventional careers, including self-employment and portfolio careers (see Chapter 12).

### Regaining control

One definition of the word 'career' is *to move in an uncontrolled direction,* as in 'The steering failed, and my car careered across the motorway.' Random movement in an uncontrolled direction. Does that sound familiar?

Job insecurity can sometimes persuades workers to keep their head down, cruise on auto-pilot for a while, and put career development on hold. The problem with this strategy arises when you come to explain your CV in a job interview. Others struggle to prove that their skills are up to date. If your CV suggests you've spent some time soft-pedalling, now might be the right time to gain new experience. You can also learn how to present your career story as a coherent narrative, a series of conscious choices ('I decided it would be better to remain in the role and see how I could develop it . . .').

## Holding out for the good stuff

When you're trying to reposition yourself in the job market, two things really help: optimism and curiosity. Optimistic thinking keeps the end in mind, encouraging you to keep pushing on doors, asking questions. Curiosity compels you to do so. Both activities radiate energy. And that's a great starting point for finding a job you love. You will need energy to fuel what might be a long slog of exploration, but energy, enthusiasm, evident motivation, and a real interest in some aspect of work – these are things that make sure you're remembered. Attitude and positive thinking need to be backed up with personal evidence. This is the practical, vital matter of expertly matching yourself to employer needs, a major theme in this book.

Whatever the state of the economy, you'll need resilience to cope with the roller-coaster of job hunting. Some current employer habits are highly frustrating for job hunters – none more so than risk-averse managers requiring candidates to attend three, four or more selection events or wait an extraordinarily long time before a final hiring decision is made. In addition, conventional job searching (see Chapter 13 on the power of unconventional methods) means you pretty much guarantee you will hear only radio silence. Attractive advertised positions are known in the recruitment industry as *candidate magnets*. Chasing them means a level of feedback that is close to zero. Many employers freely acknowledge that they don't respond to job applications unless they are inviting candidates to interview.

## Who's directing your movie?

How many times have you heard someone talking about how they have 'ended up' in a particular role? It may be time you became a director and scriptwriter.

Many people are almost entirely passive about their careers, leaving job satisfaction very much to chance. It's easy to shrug off responsibility with a phrase like *A job's a job. It pays the bills.* New occupations are opening up all the time, and people are sampling a whole range of them during the course of a single 'career'. Does this mean that people are happier in work or better at choosing career paths? It seems not. US writer Studs Terkel found that work, for some, was 'a Monday to Friday sort of dying'.

### World view *Paradigm*

*[handwritten: So if you know what else you are looking for, you get it]*

Consider for a moment your **world view** – your internal working model of how life operates. What makes up that picture? It is built from your earliest influences, memories, the world view held by your parents, and the ups and downs of life. It is often constructed as a reaction to the way that you have been treated. Your world view contains your pre-conceptions, your fears, your values. A world view is made up of sentences as well as pictures. We have an all-too familiar script running most of the time: 'charity begins at home', 'if you want a job done properly, do it yourself', 'keep your cards close to your chest'. This world is strongly influenced by the media's constant flow of bad news, but in every generation you will find people who, looking at the same evidence, can justify any world view that appeals – scarcity or abundance, conflict or cooperation, doom or hope. Look closely at the picture you hold of yourself and the script you run in your own personal soap opera. Do you see closed doors, or doors with handles?

*Ah, that depends* . . . And it does. It depends on the way you look. Look at the signals you receive during the course of a day. How many times do you receive praise and ignore it? How many times do you hear neutral or objective data and take it the wrong way? How often do you hear criticism and clutch it to yourself as the last, final, and totally accurate picture of *you*? The reality is that most of us have an impressive talent: to ignore positive information, distort neutral information, and attach ourselves to negative ideas.

There are always people who find interesting and well-paid work even when opportunities seem to be thin on the ground. Are they lucky? To a small extent. The rest is down to how they choose to think, and how they choose to act.

---

## Exercise 1.1 – Breaking out of default mode

Electronic devices have a 'default mode', often the original factory settings. When you're looking for a new job, employers, recruiters, and other contacts make assumptions about what you're looking for. For example, recruitment agencies may assume you want a similar role to the one you held most recently.

Think about the 'default mode' your career suggests, using the prompts below.

|  | What role will people expect you to undertake next in 'default mode' ... |
|---|---|
| based on your last job? |  |
| based on your career history? |  |
| based on page 1 of your CV? |  |

| based on your LinkedIn profile? | |
|---|---|
| based on your most recent qualifications or training? | |

What would you really like to do? What would you call that job?

If you can't name the job, how is it different from the 'default' jobs listed above?

## 'Must do' list

- ✓ Use a hardback notebook to jot down your discoveries and the results of the exercises in this book. Write down the steps you need to take in the next two months. Then take step one.
- ✓ Plan ahead. Look at the chapter headings and decide how and when you are going to set aside time to go through this process.
- ✓ Reflect: have your career decisions been made consciously, or have you largely responded to opportunity and chance? How much of your career is about regret or missed opportunity?
- ✓ What's the 'default' mode for your career? What will happen if you do nothing?
- ✓ Look again at your experiences of applying for jobs. What's working well for you? What could you do differently?
- ✓ Identify someone you know who has very clearly taken control of their career. Find out their first steps, how they made change happen, and how they sustain their energy.

# Barriers and blocks

'The trouble with the rat race is that even if you win, you're still a rat.'  **Lily Tomlin**

*This chapter explores the following topics:*

- The mindset that helps you avoid change
- The blocks between you and a great career
- Overcoming personal barriers
- Defining your preferred time balance in a job.

## Dealing with 'yes, but'

At this point, you may be hearing two familiar words in your head: **'yes, but . . .'**. You're in safety-first gear again. We all do it. It's your ancient brain speaking – the part attuned to avoiding risk and seeking safety. It's the senior committee member who faithfully attends every meeting in your brain and says: 'We've heard all this stuff before', 'It'll never fly', 'I'd be taking a risk', 'It might work for somebody else', 'Show me the statistics', 'It might work in London, but . . .'.

'Yes, but' thinking is the biggest block to career transition. Saying 'yes, but' is a good way of avoiding change: 'Yes, but I have to earn a living', 'Yes, but in the real world . . .'. It's often a sign that the speaker is not listening positively – it's a classic defence mechanism, a way of avoiding having to face issues.

'Yes, but' allows you to pretend that you're making a sensible decision by avoiding risk. You'll justify it using all the old phrases: 'The grass is always greener . . .',' Better the devil you know . . .'. The really dangerous result of 'yes, but' isn't avoiding big steps – it's never taking even one small one. You don't have to make a radical overnight change, and you certainly don't need to make a big decision. You just need to make one small decision: to *look*. To find out, ask questions, follow your curiosity. 'Yes, but' stops you in your tracks, ensures you fail before you've tried anything.

## Exercise 2.1 – Constraints

We all have constraints, but each of us thinks that our constraints are uniquely limiting. Tick the constraints that you feel apply to you.

| | |
|---|---|
| ☐ I am too old | ☐ I don't have many |
| ☐ I am under-qualified | achievements |
| ☐ My experience is all in one | ☐ I worry about taking risks |
| industry | ☐ Don't know what I want to |
| ☐ I have a health problem | do next |
| ☐ Location | ☐ Worry that I will be out of |
| ☐ Travel is a problem | work for a long time |
| ☐ Lack of information about | ☐ Fear of employer's attitude |
| the job market | to redundancy |
| ☐ The stigma of unemployment | ☐ Lack of up-to-date skills |
| ☐ Financial commitments | ☐ Fear of rejection |
| ☐ Family/personal problems | ☐ Lack of relevant qualifications |
| ☐ Fear of approaching people | ☐ Worry about having to |
| ☐ Lack of confidence selling | retrain/go back to full-time |
| myself in person | study |
| ☐ My job search to date hasn't | ☐ I want a job that looks good |
| worked | on my CV |
| ☐ I don't want to make the | ☐ I have never had to apply for |
| wrong decision at my time | a job before |
| of life | ☐ I don't interview well |

When you have completed the constraints exercise, look at the boxes you've ticked. Now take a highlighter and mark the top half dozen or so you think are most limiting.

Look at the constraints you can do something about, and those you can't – for example, travel-to-work limitations. Other fixed constraints might be about hours of work or minimum income levels. Knowing these fixed components can be helpful. Some constraints simply describe where you are on a learning curve: 'I don't interview well' means it's time for more practice.

Look again at your biggest constraints. When have you overcome these constraints in the past? What did you do to move beyond them? You may already know the steps you need to take to overcome these constraints again in the future.

If you feel you have constraints you can't overcome, it may be time to find help. The most powerful constraints are psychological, such as 'I don't want to make the wrong decision at my time of life'. These thoughts are not just ideas – they limit your performance. You can spot these constraints a mile off – one-liners that pop into your head when you consider something risky, or thoughts that keep you awake at 2 am. (If they do, don't act on them. Psychologists tell us that the voice you hear in your head in the small hours of the morning is a child's voice, speaking from fear. Things usually look different in the morning.)

### Personal barriers, and creative ways to overcome them

As Exercise 2.1 shows, some important barriers are external; most arise from the way you see things. Here are some of the most common:

**Lack of confidence.** The key to getting an ideal job lies as much in your confidence as in your skills or the state of the labour market. Seek out positive feedback and record it somewhere so you can retrieve it when you feel low. Resist every temptation to put yourself down.

**Fear of making mistakes.** The world's greatest inventions are the result of mistakes. Mistakes are simply feedback on our performance. Winners make far more mistakes than losers – they get more feedback as they continue to try out more possibilities. The more timid mind stops after one mistake. Thomas Edison failed to invent the light bulb several thousand times before coming up with a version that worked. IBM chief Thomas Watson once said: 'The way to succeed is to double your failure rate.'

**Fear of rejection.** Statistically you will be rejected more times than you are accepted. This is a fact of life, not a reflection of what you have to offer. The positive career changer looks at every interview, every discussion, as a learning opportunity. The most important question is, 'What did I learn from this?' If you find yourself thinking, 'all I learned was that people don't want me', then look again.

**I don't know if I want the job.** Research, and find out. Compare your 'I wish' list to the employer's 'We want' list. If it seems right, throw yourself at the opportunity with enthusiasm. If there are difficult decisions to make about moving house, or whatever, don't worry about them until the job offer is actually in your hand.

**Fear of boasting.** Some people feel embarrassed describing their own strengths and successes. Boasting is when you come to the conclusion that you have something better than everyone else, and ram it down their throats. Discovering your true skills, talents, and attributes is about learning to be at peace with the way you are. In some cultures, the idea of the 'tall poppy' means that people avoid being seen as distinctive or having particular achievements. The result is that no one knows what you can really do.

**No achievements.** Everybody has achievements, but some people choose not to recognise them. It's all relative. It is part of human nature to have goals and to overcome obstacles. The point is to recognise your achievements and to celebrate them, rather than assume they are of little worth and of no interest to others.

**No clear direction.** You might assume that you can't begin working on your career without knowing where you're going. Set out to discover options, and decide later. Don't keep telling people 'I'm not sure what I want yet.' Celebrate the fact that you are exploring. Employers are not interested in hearing about your uncertainty – they want to know how you can help solve their problems.

**Image.** Find as many ways as you can to improve your own self-image (see the paragraph on lack of confidence above), but also learn to see how the world sees you. Ask your friends how they and others perceive you; most people find this feedback rather surprising.

**Self-criticism** can be helpful and is sometimes painful, but should be a short-term burst of activity, not a way of life. The human brain is finely attuned to giving out negative messages, and we all gravitate towards our dominant thoughts. If you keep telling yourself 'I'll never be a manager', you will subconsciously use every ounce of energy to make sure this becomes a self-fulfilling truth.

**The shock of the new.** It takes courage to make dramatic career changes, and courage to throw yourself into an entirely new job. Try to remember times in your past when you made similar leaps. How long, in fact, was your adjustment period? We are actually quite good at adjusting to new conditions. Even the most demanding and strange environment can become familiar and routine within a matter of months.

**The expectations of others.** Don't let other people live your career for you. Everyone does it: parents, teachers, friends, colleagues. They paint a picture of the future (based on scant information) and you feel obliged to live it out. You need two kinds of people to make these decisions properly: (a) skilled professionals who can help you to identify where your career is going; and (b) a core team of supporters who can positively encourage you to make it happen.

**Lack of information.** Many people try to imagine what new sectors (sometimes described as fields of work) will be like. Imagination can be a helpful step in reaching a goal, but solid information is out there – and easy to grasp. Talk to people who are currently doing the job. Find out what a job feels like from the inside.

**Be careful what you ask for.** One peculiarity of the brain is that we attract what we fear. You see a small child carrying a bowl of cereal and say, 'Careful you don't spill that.' What happens? You shift the child's focus from carrying to spilling, and the bowl tips. If you concentrate on the things you fear, you unconsciously put energy into negative outcomes. It sounds corny, but there really is power in positive thinking.

**No goals.** Start with small goals – and stick to them. Plan your week ahead: find someone to take out for coffee so you can explore ideas and practise talking about your work history.

**Protect your ideas for the future.** New ideas need 'greenhousing' – when we have new ideas, sometimes the worst thing we can do is to share them with the wrong kind of people and have them dismissed or trashed. Cultivate ideas quietly and share them with positive-minded people.

Watch for **drains and radiators.** Some people around you are *drains*, who absorb your energy; others are *radiators*, who push energy out. Radiators will say 'go for it'. Drains say 'that will never work'. Drains tell you to be 'realistic', which usually means doing next to nothing in the hope that something else will come along.

Watch your **energy levels.** As you begin exploring, your enthusiasm is high. It can easily flag – often when you hit the first obstacle. Plan *now* to talk to someone positive at that critical time. Get other people to make you accountable for your short-term goals.

**It's a dog-eat-dog world.** It's sometimes argued that competition brings out the best in products, but the worst in people. Don't make the mistake of thinking you're in competition with everyone else. You're not. You're up against the requirements of a particular job and the needs of a particular employer.

## Problems for the career doctor

Time to discuss your various 'yes, but' symptoms. The career doctor will see you now.

### The jobs aren't there

You might feel there are few jobs available. Finding a job you love for at least half the week can seem hard if you aren't seeing vacancies. As Chapter 1 reveals, jobs are increasingly off-radar. Every day people leave jobs or retire and new roles are created, and exciting roles can be found even when employers don't seem to be hiring or the economy is going through uncertain times. What's important is this: *the economy isn't in your head.* If it dictates every choice, every action, your reaction to every opportunity, then you're buying in to the majority view that it's not worth exploring.

### Too long in the same job

The 'same job' could have been a 20-year history of change, variety, and development. We're not demotivated by being in one job or one organisation. We're turned off when things start repeating themselves and we're not learning or changing.

Even if you're in a great job that you love doing, you may not want to do it forever. Most careers need a reboot from time to time.

### The side benefits are good

In one firm, an employee stayed on for several years because somebody brought in an excellent cake every day. We all have our reasons for staying. If you find yourself saying, 'The pension scheme/the medical insurance/the gym is so good . . .', then the question should be: *but is this why I'm here?* Side benefits evaporate quickly when organisations cut costs. When your last day on earth arrives, are you going to say 'I wish my pension had been just a bit bigger' or 'Why did I waste 20 years in that office watching the clock?'

### I'll stick at it

'The job's okay, and a lot of things are good about it, and even though it's boring, it's a good place to ride out the storm . . .'. There are a lot of people in the workplace today who are thinking that way. The problem is that dull jobs create dull people. Once your learning curve has flattened out and the job is no longer challenging, you've made a strange pact with yourself: *I will trade boredom for security.* This may mean future problems explaining your CV choices.

### I don't want to make the wrong decision

Hoping for a low-risk career, a job that will take you safely through to retirement, is a hopeless longing for work to be like it was in the 1960s. We have to take more career decisions

for ourselves, and the fear of getting them wrong can be disabling. Being motivated to *avoid* danger can means that your energy goes into avoiding the first steps of exploration. Incremental thinking only gets you incremental results. Change happens when you do at least one thing differently.

### I just need a job

You may by now have concluded that creative career management might be good for other people, not you. You feel you've got to deal with a hard reality. You need something right now, that pays the bills. This might be because you are unemployed, or because you are not paid enough to make ends meet. This makes you vulnerable in the labour market. It may persuade you to become a 'job beggar', with your hat in your hand, saying: 'I'll do anything.' That's a great way to avoid being hired.

Some years ago I worked with a group of job seekers from one of the townships in Johannesburg. One of them, Gugu, was aged seventeen and had given up looking for work. Why? 'There are no jobs in South Africa,' she said. But new jobs are being created in that country every day. 'Yes, but so many people are chasing them,' she said sadly. Talking to her I realised that all over the world too many people fall into job-beggar mode. Fortunately, Gugu and her fellow job seekers all found jobs – as a result of a programme encouraging them to focus on their strengths and share them with employers.

### No, it's true: I just need a job

If you take the first thing that comes along, how are you going to explain that when your CV is scrutinised in years to come? Right now you might be thinking, '*there are no choices*'. Just get some perspective on that statement. Compared with most of the world's population, past and present, people in today's developed world have a huge range of life choices, and more protection against failure. We all have choices. Some people find brilliant jobs even in the depths of a recession. During 2018, more people were employed in the UK than at any time in its history, yet you could still hear people saying, 'This is a really bad time to be looking for a new job.'

Perhaps an inner voice is saying, 'get *real* – looking for an enjoyable job is self-indulgence, a daydream'. How many excuses do you need to have to ensure you stay miserable at work? Listen to successful people talking about the work they do. They don't often say 'Well, the money's good.' They talk about work being like a 'game', being 'fun', or they talk about the privilege of doing for a living what they would gladly do for nothing. Alternatively, if you need a practical reason for not taking just any job, it's this: in five years' time, how will you explain this job on your CV?

Effective career planning is about finding a job that works for you, matching who you are to the life you are going to lead. That's not a luxury, not a fantasy: it's your choice of reality.

### I can't move on

It's all too easy to believe that the only solution to unhappiness at work is job change. Often, all that work dissatisfaction can show you is that there's a mismatch between who you are and what you are doing. That mismatch shows, if not to ourselves, to others. But the real answer is **career growth**: moving towards a closer match between yourself and the work you do. Career growth may be something you can achieve exactly where you are already. Review your current job carefully and ask yourself:

- If I could change something using a magic wand, would it be the people, the place, the rewards, the tasks I do?

- What parts of the job do I enjoy?
- What parts do I *really* enjoy? When does the time pass quickly?

Make a list, then be clear about what you can change, and what you can't.

### I'm too old

Yes, employers are wrong-headed about age. But time and time again they buy experience, know-how, reliability. Employers sometimes assume that younger people are more adaptable and have more stamina, but they also recognise that older workers are often more committed, more reliable, and come with more common sense. I recommend Denise Taylor's book *You're Hired! Find Work at 50+* (Trotman, 2016). In the foreword I wrote about the fact that some organisations are very evidently 'young' cultures, where it can be hard for older workers to break in. Some employers do of course have an unenlightened view of older workers, who can of course offer important characteristics, including wisdom, reliability, and staying power.

Match what you have to offer against the job carefully, and be careful that you don't build age barriers in the way you present yourself. All too many older workers draw attention to their age by apologising for it or talking about how things 'used to be done'. Some take an odd pride in making statements like *'I don't do this social media stuff.'* Age matters if that's the main focus of the information you present, especially if you don't emphasise the fact that you're a great fit for the job and a mature, safe pair of hands.

Employers who discriminate on the grounds of age are either too young to appreciate that anyone can have an original idea over the age of 30 (so show them . . .) or old and tired and assume that everyone over 40 is equally old and tired. If the employer wants a 21-year-old he or she can burn out in two years, do you want to be there anyway?

### I don't have the qualifications

Formal qualifications are often less relevant than people think. There are so many degrees, diplomas, and certificates that employers can't tell one from another, and they have little idea if any predict workplace performance.

In the (rarer than you might think) event that a particular qualification is a stated requirement, then ask yourself, 'why do they need this? – what problem will it solve?' For many roles, relevant experience is often an acceptable alternative. Talk about what you know and what you can do: make your answers specific to the problems posed in this job.

### I don't have the money to retrain

Almost every journalist seeking career change tips asks, 'Don't people have to retrain?' Most of us assume that career change means full-time learning. Look for alternative ways in. Don't let 'I'd need to retrain' become a job myth that stops you finding out. Is there something you can learn in your own time? If you think you need a specific qualification, find out it if it will improve your employability or just put a hole in your bank balance.

### I'm not IT-literate

At one time using a computer was considered a specialised skill. Now under-fives do it. It's not rocket science. If you say *I'm not online,* an employer assumes you don't care about the way work is done today. Get connected, and check your email at least once a day.

There are a million things the web makes easier: research, finding people to speak to, discovering new ideas, tracking down former colleagues, seeking recommendations and endorsements. Trying to achieve these outcomes without using the internet is rather like trying to cook a three-course meal over a candle flame – an unnecessary challenge providing indifferent results very, *very* slowly.

### I'll never earn what I earn here

This one's the kiss of death, because it's really saying: 'I'm overpaid here, and no other employer will let me get away with it.' This is usually wrong-headed. Few people stay overpaid for long. If you're making a big hole in the payroll and not delivering much in return, this is a good time to rethink your role.

### I might be found out

It's surprising how many people in senior jobs share a common fear: they are pretending to be good enough, and one day they'll be found out. This is the **impostor syndrome**, first recognised in the 1970s, and widely experienced. Many people believe they got a job through luck and they are fakes. Their secret fear is that one day their boss will say: 'OK, we know it's been a big pretence. Just leave now and we'll say nothing more about it.' A worrying number of people would leave the building without protest.

Insecurity is everywhere. The strange thing is that most workers assume that top-level bosses are immune to it. In fact, many senior staff are so isolated they spend more energy than anyone else coping with feeling like an impostor.

### *I don't interview well*

Absolute statements like this set you up to fail. Start with small steps: catalogue what you've done and learn how to talk about it. Read Chapter 16.

## Exercise 2.2 – Time balance

How would you like to spend your time at work? What would be the ideal time balance?

Think about your current or most recent job. In the left-hand column, estimate the percentage of time you spend in each kind of activity. In the right-hand column, state your preferred time allocation, again as a percentage. Each column should add up to 100.

| Actual % | Activity | Preferred % |
|---|---|---|
| | **Working entirely alone**<br>Working on my own without distraction. Working things out, being given space to sort out a problem or finish a piece of work, writing something, having time to reflect . . . | |
| | **Working independently but close to colleagues**<br>Being responsible for own results but having colleagues around. Having ready access to the ideas and encouragement of other people . . . | |
| | **Working 1:1**<br>Explaining, persuading, influencing, selling, coaching, managing, teaching . . . | |
| | **Attending meetings**<br>Meeting to deal with agendas, share information, and make collective decisions . . . | |

| | | |
|---|---|---|
| | **Working in active teams**<br>Group problem-solving, planning, brainstorming, reviewing, getting things done, training, motivating . . . | |
| | **Extending your network**<br>Telephoning new contacts, networking, meeting new people, going to conferences, seminars . . . | |
| | **Working with an audience**<br>Public speaking, performing, entertaining, giving talks, informing larger groups . . . | |
| **100%** | Total | **100%** |

When you have completed the time balance exercise, compare your current role with your ideal. This isn't self-indulgence or fantasy – it's a healthy recognition of how you work at your best. Look at the activities where you spend most of your time. Which would you like to increase or decrease, substantially? What difference would that make to your effectiveness?

### 'Must do' list

- ✓ Career problems are sometimes concrete, but usually strategies for avoiding the issue of change. What are your favourite 'yes, but' defences?
- ✓ You can be happy at work. What is the first step you could take to achieve that? How would your friends and colleagues notice the difference?
- ✓ Look at your CV, your interview style, your attitude to work. You complain that employers see negative things about you. How many of these messages are actually composed and delivered by you? How can you reframe the way you present yourself?
- ✓ Use the time balance exercise to get a broad picture of what your ideal job would look like in terms of activities.

# 3

# Getting more out of work

'Normal is getting dressed in clothes that you buy for work, driving through traffic in a car that you are still paying for, in order to get to the job that you need so you can pay for the clothes, car and the house that you leave empty all day in order to afford to live in it.' **Ellen Goodman**

*This chapter helps you to:*

- Look at what you get out of work
- Discover what you find interesting and stimulating
- Work out how far you are from your dream job – and what you can do about it
- Think about the relationship between job satisfaction and general happiness
- Assemble your jigsaw job.

## The good, the bad, and the just plain awful

A series of reports from the Gallup organisation indicate that, worldwide, less than one in five employees are engaged at work. 'Engaged' in this context meant psychologically committed to a role – and unlikely to leave if an opportunity presented itself. Repeated Gallup surveys indicate that a large proportion of engaged US workers would continue in their jobs if they won a $10 million lottery. Clearly, work motivation is a complicated arena.

What are the things at work that give you a buzz? The sort of things you go home and talk about? Write them down – they're worth recording. Take a blank piece of paper and divide it into three columns which you can fill in as you reflect on work:

1. The really good stuff        Things you find stimulating and enjoyable

2. Things I could live without        When do you find work boring or dull?

3. Things I put up with at work that I need like a hole in the head        What aspects of work fill you with dread or loathing?

---

## Exercise 3.1 – How happy are you in your work?

Tick the box next to the description which best describes your work right now.

☐ **Dream job**

I often feel I can't wait to get into work. Work is the place where I grow and learn most, where I am set healthy challenges, where I am valued and appreciated. A great deal of fun and self-esteem is centred in my work, which fits my values, talents, and personality. I know that I make a difference. I express who I am in my job. The rewards are right, and I would be happy to be paid less if necessary. I love the part work plays in my life.

☐ **Thumbs up**

I enjoy work most of the time, but sometimes there are headaches and problems. My work feels useful and contributes to my self-esteem. My contribution is clear, acknowledged, and significant. My career is a good match to my talents, personality, and values. I am appreciated by others. I feel that I make a difference, and that I add something positive to the organisation. I find supervision helpful, but my boss is more a mentor than a supervisor. I lead a satisfying career which contributes to all parts of my life.

☐ **Mustn't grumble**

I accept the work I do. Sometimes I feel valued, other times exploited or ignored. Work is stable, largely unexciting, doesn't interfere with my inner life too much. New ways of doing things are sometimes discouraged. I may be in the right line of work, but in the wrong organisation. I am valued for some of what I do, but not always the most important things.

☐ **Someone's got to do it**

I work because I need to. I don't feel I owe a great deal to my employer. Several parts of the job are unpleasant/boring/demeaning/pointless. Real life begins at five o'clock. I'm not learning anything. I try to make a contribution but sometimes hit a brick wall. My skills are getting rusty. I would just like a quiet life.

☐ **Clock watcher**

There are days I almost have to drag myself to work; every day and every moment are miserable. I feel a huge mismatch between the person I am and the person this job requires me to be. I feel trapped. Each day makes things seem worse. I dread the prospect of Monday morning. I take all my sick leave because the job often makes me feel ill.

Consider your results from Exercise 3.1. If you're in the first category, congratulations. Recognise what's good about your work and ensure that it remains that way. Generally, only a minority of people place themselves in the top two groups. Indeed, surveys repeatedly show that at least two-thirds of people are unhappy in their work. If you're in the 'clock watcher' box, make a review of how you can change things – soon! As this chapter discusses, you don't need to aim for a dream job to make significant changes in your working life.

## Is work that important?

Judging by the amount of time spent complaining about work, it must be. If it wasn't for work, we would have far less to moan about. We put a huge amount of energy into work, and rely on it for a large chunk of our self-esteem. For this reason alone, unemployment and underemployment are damaging. Equally, people in work where they don't feel demotivated or engaged can often feel that life lacks something important. As this chapter outlines, you'll spend a great deal of time in work. Work will consume a large amount of your energy, creativity, and stamina. Therefore, one thing should be clear. Choosing the work you do is one of the most important life decisions you will ever make.

Do you *work to live* or *live to work*? If you believe that you work to live, you may be more motivated by the things you do outside work than the things which earn you a living. You are living out your dream in a different reality, and your salary is there simply to fund your dream. A lot of people live that way, and can be happy.

If you feel that you live to work, it may be that you've found the best job in the world, or perhaps you haven't explored enough to find out what life has to offer. Perhaps work plays too important a part in your life? Those who suffer the greatest impact of redundancy are those who have made their work their only focus, perhaps at the expense of family or personal development.

### What you get out of work, and what work gets out of you

My grandfather Owen Roberts had a way with words in both Welsh and English. One of his favourite expressions was *I eat well, I sleep well, and when I think about work*

*I tremble all over.* It wasn't true, of course. He spent many happy years working as a dockside blacksmith.

We sometimes enjoy complaining about work even when it's satisfying. However, there is evidence to suggest that during the past 20–30 years we have become increasingly unhappy at work, and one of the most common reasons quoted is long working hours. The charity Working Families, in its report *The Modern Families Index 2018*, recorded that 40% of UK working parents frequently put in extra working hours at home in the evenings or weekends (www. workingfamilies.org.uk). The Mental Health Foundation (www.mentalhealth.org.uk) argues that, 'The cumulative effect of increased working hours is having an important effect on the lifestyle of a huge number of people, which is likely to prove damaging to their mental well-being.'

The 2017 YouGov report *Work–Life Balance: The tools for retention* (reports.yougov.com) recorded that one in five 25–34-year-olds were 'unhappy with their work/life balance'. The report added that 'poor work–life balance can have a notable impact on employees. They tend to be more disengaged with life in general than the average person, envying their friends' lifestyles . . . and feeling alienated by modern life.'

There are other factors too: people seem to have increased expectations of what their careers will provide; others are fazed by several decades of downsizing and job uncertainty. While some people are burdened by overwork and in danger of burnout, others have too little work. It matters more than ever that you have a toolkit to help you to find a job that builds you up more than it breaks you down.

### The days of your life

If you think you can get by with a so-so job, you might be ignoring the huge amount of time that work consumes.

If you work full-time hours, you spend more of your life in work than in any other waking activity (if you live for 70 years, you'll spend about 23 of those years asleep and 16 years working). You will spend at least 100,000 hours in work. That's 'in work' – what Americans call 'face time', the time when your jacket is on the back of your chair (think about all the other hours that go into preparing for work, worrying about work, or complaining about work).

We like to think we have the power to make life choices, but for most people work is the dominating event. According to the ONS, life expectancy at birth for females born in the UK in 2016 was just above 83 years. Call it 32,000 days. Men get rather less – about 29,000 days. That's somewhere around 30,000 days to learn, work, play, raise a family, leave your mark on life, and acquire wisdom. If you get to the age of 50, on average you'll get longer than this, but even knowing that, you might think that 30,000 days doesn't sound like a lot of time, does it? Especially if you're saying, 'this isn't what I wanted to do when I grew up . . .'.

### Why should people be happy at work?

It's easy to believe that work is not somewhere you are supposed to enjoy yourself. You can easily create a world of compartments: this is the compartment where I work; this is my family compartment; this small compartment in the corner is where I really enjoy myself. It's all part of that either/or thinking we're so good at (see Chapter 4 for the games we play around 'ideal' and 'real').

Career development specialist Carole Pemberton talks about the Faustian pact we make in our careers – a deal you make that allows you to think in these either/or terms, like Faust's pact with the devil. A pact typically says 'I can only be successful if . . .'. Here are some examples: 'I can only be a top salesperson if I work long hours and eat badly'; 'I can only be a great manager if I don't empathise with my staff.' Listen to the language people use when they decide to compromise. They 'settle for' choices they're not really comfortable with. They 'lower their sights'. They pretend they are being logical and sensible.

Why should people be happy at work? Work isn't fun, your friends will tell you. Work is about hard-nosed reality. If that sounds reasonable, look again at the people who seem to have most fun in their jobs. They're often running their own businesses, making new things happen, sharing what they know, and inspiring people. Some are in jobs that directly improve the lives of others. Others are producing brilliant ideas, products or great experiences for customers. Are these workers richer or poorer as a result? Happiness and success don't always come hand in hand, but it must also be clear that being unhappy is no automatic route to success. Unfortunately, it's often the unhappy, unenthusiastic, low-energy people that companies get rid of first. Some workers are successful and paid well simply because they have found work that channels their best energy.

*Why should people be happy at work?* Take a deep breath. Read that question again. Work is where you spend most of your waking life. It's where you put about 80% of your best energy. Yes, you have energy for things outside your job, but for most of us working in what is increasingly becoming a 24/7 economy, most of your stamina, imagination, and personal energy will be expended on work. Work matters. It may be one of the things in life that contributes most to self-esteem and a sense of fulfilment. In today's world, choosing how you spend Monday to Friday is probably one of the most important life decisions you make.

So the question *why should people be happy at work?* really means *why should people be happy?* What do you think? Do happy people live longer, stay healthier, have great children, and make a difference? You know they do. So let's stop that all-time Faustian deal: 'I can only get a great job if I forget about being happy at work.' That's a self-fulfilling deal. Be careful what you ask for – you might just get it.

'One of the symptoms of an approaching nervous breakdown is the belief that one's work is terribly important.'

**Bertrand Russell**

### Happiness – goal or accident?

Are some occupations more satisfying than others? We seem to have a constant fascination with the worst jobs in society. Surveys looking at the 'best' jobs tend to look at salary, status, and job satisfaction. A recent survey put 'marketing manager' top of the list. Other benchmarks used in research point to roles such as childcare workers, clergy, and those offering personal services such as healthcare, travel, and catering. Low job satisfaction has recently been recorded among teachers, social workers, and those in the charity, retail, and health sectors.

It's worth saying a little more about happiness. Many of us think that happiness is a vague, subjective, and entirely individual state of mind. Others believe that we can do very little to influence or adjust happiness. Richard Layard's book *Happiness: Lessons from a New Science* (2011) reflects on research undertaken into what makes some communities and nations happier than others. This research begins with the principle that when people say they are generally happy or very happy in life, this is something that can be measured. Layard looks at the major factors in life that contribute to happiness – and the results are fascinating. First, being happy seems to contribute directly to good health. Second, being rich doesn't make people any happier. Many countries in the developing world with low income levels per capita are just as content as developed nations, and in some cases happier. Career coaches know that job satisfaction is often not directly related to gaining a pay rise. Internationally, as Layard writes, 'higher average income is no guarantee of greater happiness'.

Such thinking has major consequences for career planning. First, there is a relationship between money and happiness in terms of being underpaid or not having enough. If you are not earning enough to pay your bills or working long hours to achieve pay less than your peers, long-term dissatisfaction is likely to follow. It's also worth thinking about other factors which contribute to long-term happiness, including mental and physical health, family relationships, friendships, and the feeling of belonging to a community. Many people find that happiness comes from helping others. Money aside, work plays a part in many other ways – being unemployed or underemployed often damages self-esteem. Layard is among many who point out that fulfilling work is an important aspect of happiness, especially where you have some control over how you work (see 'independence' among the Career Hot Buttons in Chapter 6).

## Getting more excited about the 9 to 5

Careers specialists have long talked about *motivated skills* – the skills you relish using. There's a big difference between doing something because you know how, and doing it because it feels worth doing. That difference is the power of motivation. Motivation turns an errand into a quest, a task into a joy. You'll read more about skills in Chapter 7.

Career exploration depends on the motivation you apply to the process. *You get out what you put in.* Read that last sentence again. Your success in gaining a stunning career depends as much on your own personal motivation as it does on any other combination of factors, internal or external. And that's not all. Some of the satisfaction you will get from career exploration and success will be about meeting other people, finding out about them, making connections, and – occasionally – helping others out. So here's an important reminder in a rather self-focused age: one of the strongest factors affecting happiness is the opportunity to help other people.

## Exercise 3.2 – Your Jigsaw Job

People sometimes find it hard to describe their ideal job. This exercise allows you to think about work without getting locked into a job title or sector.

Imagine that you buy a jigsaw puzzle from a charity shop, but the puzzle comes in a plastic bag: you have no box, no picture, no title. You don't know if the picture shows a cottage, a seascape or a kitten. You adopt new roles to begin assembling the jigsaw. Perhaps you begin with the edges and corners. You let go of the question 'What is this a picture of?'

Start by imagining you're in a fulfilling job. Don't worry what the job is called or what it says on your business card. Start with a feeling – you enjoy the job. When you're planning for work on a Sunday afternoon, you anticipate the working week positively. You've been in the role for at least 12 months and it's still stimulating. The first question is around location and setting. Imagining yourself in this 'virtual' role, what do you see around you?

Look at the example below. The right-hand side shows one client's answers. Copy out topics from the left-hand column, then write down your own answers to build up your own jigsaw job.

| Topic | Example response |
|---|---|
| Location, setting | Urban. Aesthetically pleasing building in multicultural centre. Good light. The role involves travel and meeting people |
| Hours | The opportunity to work from home about once a week |
| People | A role where I have a mentor. Trusting, cooperative environment. To be part of an enthusiastic, smart team – sharing ideas, thinking collectively |
| The way I manage other people | More a mentor than a supervisor. I like people I can rely on to do the job without being chased |
| The way I am managed | My boss is direct, honest, sees my potential. Keeps me on the straight and narrow but gives me freedom to perform tasks in my own way |
| Skills I use | Being the face of the organisation. Liaising, explaining; translating complex ideas into straightforward terms. Communicating/influencing. Using creative and analytical thinking |
| Problems | Trying to help people with their problems. Completing work on time |
| Challenges | Competition: something to drive me. The job is testing/stretching. Learning about managing/leadership |
| Values expressed | Strong ethos. Clear sense of purpose/ meaning |
| Likely/attractive outcomes include | Getting a team result. Bringing the best out of people. Delighting the client |
| General details | A firm that's large enough to help me grow, small enough to support people |

| The job will be rewarding because . . . | I will be achieving something. It will be fun |
|---|---|
| How work contributes to life outside work | Comfortable lifestyle. Health. Well-being |
| Work will allow time and energy for me to do these things outside work | Spending time with family and friends. Enjoying the theatre and cultural events again |

## 'Must do' list

- ✓ Reflect on how big a part work plays in your life, and how much it contributes to your general sense of well-being.
- ✓ Examine your work–life balance. How much of you does work require? How much energy is left for other things you'd like to do with your time?
- ✓ Consider: what combination of factors in your jigsaw job would improve your long-term job satisfaction?
- ✓ Identify someone you know who has very clearly taken control of their career. Find out their first steps, how they made change happen, and how they sustain their energy.

**4**

# First steps towards a new career deal

*This chapter helps you to:*

- Look at the mix of accident, luck, and design in your career
- Understand that a new career direction will probably require new kinds of thinking
- Learn how to work smarter rather than harder at shaping your career
- Imagine possibilities for change.

## Real and ideal

Career management sounds complicated, but it's really about starting a process. You begin by looking at yourself, discovering the work you will find most stimulating. You might think about your goals – financial, learning or personal. You'll consider life–work balance – making room for learning, family, relationships, and other activities that matter.

Having looked at yourself, you look at your environment. Career management doesn't always mean job hunting. Sometimes you might want to learn something new, or renegotiate your current role so you do more of the things that energise you. However, the process can never be entirely focused on you. A career connects you to the world around you. You will look at opportunities out there in the market, some of them job-shaped. This process involves discovering work sectors (including jobs you didn't know existed) where you can make a difference. And, as you look, you might start to imagine what you might do next.

## Exercise 4.1 – If all jobs paid the same . . .

Ask yourself the following question: 'If all jobs paid the same, what would I do for a living?'

Mull over that question for a while, then fill in the four clouds below. You don't have to complete them in order.

In an ideal world I'd like to...

What I would enjoy about it...

Qualities I would bring to this role

Skills I would LOVE to use or learn...

Reflect on your answers to Exercise 4.1. How did you feel when you were faced with the first empty cloud? What was easy? What was difficult? For career coaches this exercise provides a great deal of information about confidence, optimism, imagination – but also about what gets in the way – the constraints and 'yes, buts' that act like lead weights on a soul hungry for flight.

I often use this exercise with groups of people because it quickly reveals the prevailing mindset in the room. Some people will be energised by what they write, while others find it difficult to commit their thoughts to paper. A small minority tell me it's unrealistic. And that's partly what this exercise is about, to reveal where each person sits on the Ideal vs. Real spectrum. Think of it as a see-saw:

Where do you sit on the see-saw most of the time? In a typical job search, people start out optimistic, believing in opportunity. It takes only a few rejections to push them towards the right-hand side. This can easily be accentuated when others push job advertisements under your nose, recommending that you apply for things you know you will find dull. However optimistic we feel, there is a great deal of weight on the 'real' end of the see-saw. People talk about having a 'reality check'. They will tell you to be 'realistic'.

### Being 'realistic'

Let's look at 'realistic', the most dangerous word in the career-changer's vocabulary.

Listen to everyday career conversations going on around you in coffee shops. Someone asks the question, 'what are you looking for?' and the answer often begins, 'Well, in an ideal world . . .'. As the thought develops, watch the body language change and the voice grow downbeat. Whether voiced or not, a presence stalks: that word 'realistic'. First, you talk about an interesting 'ideal' world where work might be fun. Then your focus shifts to a rather less exciting option, a compromise – something that feels like trading down.

Under pressure, we like to make choices simple. We fall back on either/or thinking – trying to make choices easier by turning a multicoloured world into black and white. So, as with the overheard coffee shop career discussion, you might find yourself using one of the nation's favourite polarising statements: *I either find a job I enjoy doing, or (to be more realistic), I find a job that pays the bills.* That sentence sounds like an internal debate, but it isn't. The decision has already been made. You're going to be 'realistic'.

Let's be clear, there are problems at both ends of the seesaw. If you stay entirely in the Ideal zone, you're probably aiming at the kind of role that only comes up once in every thousand vacancies, or pushing on doors that are likely to stay closed. Advice which says 'just dream the dream' or 'you can be anything you want to be' doesn't cut it, even in a buoyant market. Are you looking at a likely career path (something you can and will do something about), or a daydream? On the other hand, the 'ideal' end of the spectrum is the place where you will be enthusiastic. A little bit of idealism gives you the energy you need to ask questions and seek out interesting people. It's hard to generate enthusiasm for opportunities which are simply 'realistic', ordinary, vanilla. If you follow your friends' advice and stay 'realistic', how motivated will you be to keep on looking when things don't go so well? If you're applying for a job which is uninspiring, how much energy is likely to go into your interview performance?

Back to our Ideal/Real see-saw. Imagine a number score under it:

| 'IDEAL' | | | | | | | | | | 'REAL' |
|---|---|---|---|---|---|---|---|---|---|---|
| 0 | 1 | 2 | 3 | 4 | 5 | 6 | 7 | 8 | 9 | 10 |

Where are you now in your thinking? Your score may reflect how positive you're feeling. However, if you want to feel motivated by the task, keeping somewhere to the left of the mid-point helps. A score of around 4 balances enthusiasm with pragmatism. This means you're looking at career ideas that provoke curiosity, meeting people you find interesting. You look forward to the next conversation, and you have questions you want to ask. You get a sense that the work on offer is a fairly good match to who you are. Forget the bad press that 'ideal' receives, and all those people who tell you not to waste time looking for your dream role. You're looking for *good* rather than *perfect*.

So-called 'realistic' thinking can stop you at the first hurdle, especially if applied too early in the process. The word *realistic* is dangerous – because it is rarely about what is real. It's usually second-hand information – someone else's picture of the world. Don't fall for the idea that 'realistic' means 'objective, well informed, based on reality'. Whose reality? Listen to the people who are telling you to 'lower your sights'. What does that say about their own life experience and ambitions? As Chapter 2 outlined, it really pays to spend time with positive-minded people.

Optimism equals energy, and energy matters if you want to change career – you'll need it to sustain you, and you'll need to communicate it to potential employers.

### Reality check

The above paragraphs do *not* mean that your next move should be made without any reference to the real world of employers and hiring decisions. A proper reality check means finding out what's out there, and how you match your evidence so you get shortlisted. It's equally important to be objective about lack of progress. One rejection letter is a random event. Collect information, not hunches. So, if half a dozen seasoned recruitment consultants tell you there are absolute barriers to getting shortlisted, or you discover from several contacts that a sector is in terminal decline, or that your CV as it stands will prevent you getting shortlisted, that's useful, hard data. Everything else is just random noise.

This book asks you to think about dream jobs in order to see what attracts you to real jobs. Instead of looking for perfection, look for a role offering a healthy mix of the things that keep you motivated. 'Compromise' doesn't mean defeat – it can mean a healthy working understanding:

*All work is a deal*

*between what you want out of life*

*and what an employer*

*wants out of you.*

It's useful to start to think about career choice as a deal, because that means you can let go of the idea of the perfect job, and start to think about *healthy* compromise.

### Aim for 70%

Once you know what you're looking for, try to resist offers that really don't match (read about the high/low game in Chapter 13). Aim for a good overlap, and let go of the idea of the perfect job. Believing that only 100% will do is in fact a great excuse to stop looking. Understand that work is all about making deals, and *good enough* can work for you.

Look at yourself until you're pretty sure about the kind of role that suits you best, and the skills you'd like to use. Many chapters in this book will help you with this, and you can summarise your findings on one page in the **Master Sheet** (see Appendix 1, p. 273).

Next, look at jobs that might be available to you. Compare what you want with an employer's shopping list. This means going way beyond job descriptions – dig deep to find out what the organisation needs and wants. When you know this clearly (it will usually involve at least one conversation with someone who knows the organisation well), look for overlap between you and the job:

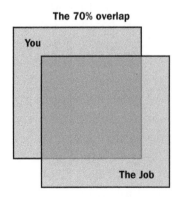

**The 70% overlap**

If you identify a genuine overlap of around 70%, the job is probably a good match – you'll be happy in work about 3½ days out of 5, which is plenty. If it feels more like 50% or 60%, the role may be an acceptable stepping stone. If the match is 50% or less, watch out.

## Working smarter rather than harder at career-building

Some say the perfect job is out there looking for you. However, you can't sit at home and wait for it to drag you out of bed. The majority of us have to rely on a mix of active investigation, supportive contacts, and luck. Luck has been described as two mathematical laws working together: chance and averaging. We can't control chance, but we can increase the odds in our favour. Invest in your future. Use thinking time carefully, and learn to think openly, because a moment's inspiration can sometimes take you much further than a year's dull planning.

Setting objectives is a vital part of the process. Ideas without activity are daydreams. The danger is that we move into activity too quickly – without really taking the opportunity to review or reinvent. Equally likely, we may continue to have career daydreams without making the first step to find out anything at all about the possibility of change. You don't need to wait for a brilliant career idea, a lucky breakthrough, or great contacts (although any of the last three will shorten the process). What you do need is to plan to take one step, soon, and then take the step after that. That's how change happens.

Information is neutral. It's easy to put all your attention on things you believe you lack. For example, 'I can't . . .', 'I've never been good at . . .', and so on. You may discover you are really good at hanging on to these ideas, and stating them as absolute facts. Exploring is an opening-out process. We tend to think along tramlines, moving logically from one stage to the next. Divergent thinking works rather differently. Let your imagination fan out: rather than making decisions too soon, look at possibilities. Try on ideas.

### *Capturing energy*

Where you put your energy matters – both in terms of exploring and job hunting. In the first phase, energy translates into attention. How do you choose to see the process of discovery? If your attention goes into believing that little is available and you have few skills to offer, that dark picture absorbs your energy. In other words, if you feel your glass is half empty, you're giving attention to absence. Soon you end up talking about all the doors that are closed to you. On the other hand, you can choose to put your energy into seeing the glass as half full. That way you start to see possibilities, perhaps even abundance – and you see it everywhere. I love the strapline used by the Australasian car hire firm Jucy: 'The glass is half full – and the other half was delicious.'

Look for organisations, sectors, products, and roles that spark your curiosity; you have a natural hunger to find out more. You find yourself talking enthusiastically about your discoveries to friends. If the ideas and people you encounter energise you, that keeps you active and reinforces the small bursts of confidence you need to pick up the phone, make connections, to keep looking even when initial results are unpromising.

This same energy matters when you're hunting for a job. Employers buy into what they describe as drive and attitude – they prefer motivated people. So, talk enthusiastically about the work sectors you've been investigating. That's step one. Step two is even more important. Look at moments in your work history where you have felt motivated. When you write and talk about your past, your task is essentially to 'bottle energy' – to capture the excitement and motivation you originally felt and communicate it. In your CV examples reveal what stimulated and enlivened you. At interview tell short, energised stories. Bottling energy is a great way of getting remembered (see 'Telling tales' in Chapter 16).

### *Career transition diamond*

Look at the **career transition diamond** below. The first phase of career transition is the lower triangle – this is all about opening out, experimentation, and idea-building. It's important not to find early reasons to say 'no' to ideas during this phase. After proper investigation you gain enough information to start closing things down. For example, you might decide to target a small number of sectors for investigation (see the exercises in Chapter 10). Now you're in the top triangle, which closes down helpfully, a time when you make choices and move towards specific outcomes.

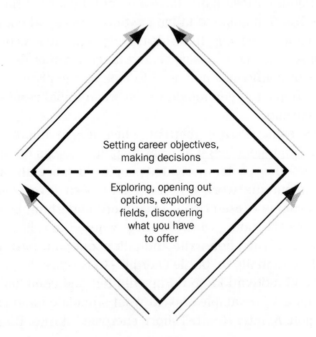

Setting career objectives, making decisions

Exploring, opening out options, exploring fields, discovering what you have to offer

Look at the **career transition diamond** again. Note the dashed line that separates the two triangles. Watch out for this important transition zone. This line marks a turning point between reflection and action – the moment you stop examining yourself and your ideas, and start to look outward at sectors, organisations, and jobs. Instead of hunting through this book for more career exercises, this will be the moment when you pick up the phone and arrange your first exploratory discussion (see Chapter 15 on information interviews).

## Exercise 4.2 – Paths not taken

Think of your career path to date. Think about paths not taken.

Consider the most important turning points in your life to date – moments when you had to choose between alternative possibilities, to decide on a particular path. Record a number of key turning points as below:

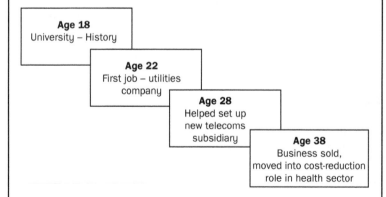

Look at **one** of your selected turning points. Write it in a box in the middle of a piece of paper. Then draw out your **paths not taken.**

**These are the alternative choices which were on offer at the time** – things you nearly did or could have done. Your final diagram might look like the following example:

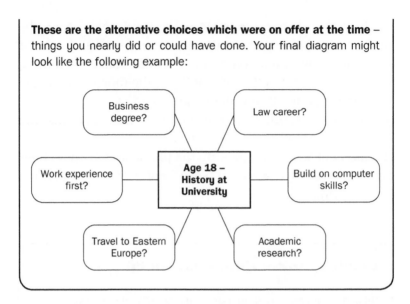

*Paths not taken – questions to ask yourself*

- What choices were available to you at this turning point?
- How did you choose the path to take?
- How have you made career decisions since?
- What difference would a change of path have made to you?
- Where have you adapted your career direction?

### Recruit a support team

A critic writing about Jane Austen suggested that the author saw two kinds of individuals: people who live and *people who see themselves living.* People who make conscious decisions about their working lives are likely to be more successful and more satisfied. They have thought about the work that they want to do and are actively pursuing it. Some have moved into new roles, and others have redesigned or renegotiated the jobs that they do.

Few things are achievable without the right tools and the right people, yet all too many job seekers try to manage careers alone. Get support. First of all, have experimental, 'what if?' conversations with as many folk as you can who can give you a different perspective (but make sure the feedback is at least objective, and preferably upbeat). Second – and do this before you finish this book – build a support team.

Find *two* other people who will help. They don't need to be in the same situation as you, but they do need to be curious about people, jobs, and the world. One other person will do, at a push, but a coach–pupil relationship often results when there are only two people. With a trio meeting together regularly, you get two perspectives on everything that's said. The conversation doesn't need to be just about you – you can help each other in turn. You'll often find that a trio discussion over a cup of coffee or a bottle of wine works very nicely.

Recruit the two members of your trio carefully. They should be people who can:

- Support you in the ups and downs of career transition.
- Give you honest, objective advice about your skills, and help you to see the evidence you use to back them up.
- Provide ideas for exploration and connections with other people who can help.
- Use 'yellow hat' thinking (see p. 59) to support your ideas. If you say 'I'm thinking of becoming an astronaut', these will be the sort of people who will say 'How could you find out more? How can you get to speak to someone who's been into space . . .?'

**Warning:** if you hear a friend say 'yes, but, in the real world . . .' or 'it's not that simple . . .' or even 'that won't work', don't invite them to be part of this process. There are thousands of people out there who will be all too happy to pour cold water on your ideas. Career success is as much about motivation as it is about strategy. Choose people who will give you encouraging feedback and positive support.

## 'Must do' list

- ✓ Reflect on what the word 'realistic' means for you. How much of your picture of work is based on second-hand or out-of-date information? What can you do to find out more?
- ✓ Work out what kind of career deal works best for you. What are the 'must have' ingredients in a new job? What can you live without?
- ✓ When you're considering a new role, find out what the job is really like, and see how far the reality of the role overlaps with your personal wish list.
- ✓ Don't get too obsessed with your CV, your interview answers, your networking 'pitch'. You get a lot more by discovering new organisations and finding out the different career deals on offer.

# Thinking around corners

'No one can persuade another to change. Each of us guards a gate of change that can only be opened from the inside. We cannot open the gate of another, either by argument or by emotional appeal.' **Marilyn Ferguson**

*This chapter looks at the following areas:*

- Exploring how you make career decisions
- Breaking out of A to Z thinking
- Letting go of the urge to decide
- Avoiding passivity and negative reinforcement
- Idea-building and moving forward towards positive solutions.

## I can't decide what kind of career I want . . .

Some decisions are easier than others. If it's obvious what job should appear next on your CV, it doesn't take much thought to name it. Other decisions are much harder, especially if you have no idea what you want to do next, can't see a way out of where you are now, or know where you want to be but don't know how to get there.

The most demanding question you'll ever hear from a career coach is not 'what would you like to do next?', but *'how are you going to decide?'* Most people secretly believe that the answer will come along if they take a test, read a book, or just sit at home with the curtains closed and think really, really hard.

### The limitations of A to Z thinking

How can you solve the problem of your career? Your instinct will probably be to use thinking strategies you've used before – analysing, categorising, researching, and planning. You want to know where you are going and plan how to get there. You'll make lists, write out pros and cons. That's a sound, business-like way of working things out, isn't it?

When you need to imagine possibilities and navigate unknown territory, A to Z thinking is not much use – lists, plans, diagrams, and flowcharts don't work. In any event, many people don't read life that way. We're inspired by conversations, by people, by stories and poems, by movies; our natural creativity needs a different kind of kick-start.

Process thinking works fine if you have a clear goal in mind, but if you really want to explore alternatives, it's inappropriate. The problem is that it leads to passivity: 'I'll get my act together when I know what I am looking for.' Finding exciting career options means setting out on a journey without a road map or a destination.

## Become an ideas factory

Don't confuse decision-making with idea-generation. You may find that you consider new ideas for a moment or two and then find a reason to say no to them, usually drawing on one of your favourite absolute statements such as 'I'm too old' (see Chapter 2 on constraints). Act on career ideas rather than just finding evidence to shoot them down. Avoid saying 'no' because there is no reason to say 'yes'. You're not deciding on your future, just exploring – playing with ideas, following where your curiosity takes you. It all starts with your imagination, then a set of questions, and then the vital step is to find people to answer those questions. Where you find something that really gets your attention, take that motivation seriously: look further, keep asking questions. That motivation doesn't just persuade you to keep pushing on doors, it's what gets you remembered.

### Thinking in different colours

Expand your range of thinking styles. Edward de Bono offers us **six thinking hats** (see www.edwarddebonofoundation. com/Creative-Thinking-Techniques). His tool has been widely adopted to ensure a wide range of thinking styles are used in decision-making. This approach also helps if you're trying to think about career options. For example, sometimes it's important to be honest about your feelings, especially where you fear change. Fear can often lead us to dismiss new ideas without exploring them at all. There are certainly times when you need simply to collect information objectively.

One of the real strengths of De Bono's coloured thinking hats is the distinction he makes between generating fresh ideas ('green hat') and a more developed process ('yellow hat') that takes ideas further, looking at potential benefits. In career terms, this means that instead of dismissing ideas as unrealistic, spend some time asking yourself 'how could I make this work? What could come out of this?'

### Get more out of your ideas

'The best way to get a good idea is to get lots of ideas.'
**Linus Pauling**, Nobel Prize-winning scientist

The word 'creative' is often over-used in the business world, but clichés have their usefulness. 'Thinking outside the box' was a term used in the advertising industry to think outside the rectangular frame of an advertising billboard. 'Pushing the envelope' comes from the field of aviation. The 'envelope' is the box-like shape on a graph representing an aeroplane's maximum speed and range. Behind the tired language lie some highly useful concepts.

Try describing your next career idea in terms that sound nonsensical. Perhaps you'd like to explore 'a sector which is about persuading and influencing but avoids people', or you might want to 'build houses that nobody will live in'. Try the Idea Grid below, or look at what happens when you combine interesting sectors (see Exercise 10.2 – From subjects of interest to occupational sectors). Try turning your sector upside down. For example, you may be interested in child development because you are interested in the way young people grow. Turning that upside down might lead you to thinking about the effects of ageing.

Here are some suggestions for idea-building:

- Allow yourself to generate a range of ideas, without self-criticism.
- If you feel your brain is overloaded, do something entirely different – run up a hill, watch a movie, cook. Putting your brain in a new gear is often a great way of generating ideas.
- When a new idea hits you, don't dismiss it as daydreaming. Test it out.
- Don't restrict yourself to tools that you find easiest or the most comfortable. Stretch yourself.
- *Do* something with every career idea – turn it into a piece of research or a conversation.

## Be more experimental

Enjoy finding out, and stop worrying about making a decision. That doesn't mean avoiding taking action, or avoiding choice in the long term, but recognising that most experiments don't lead to instant success. Experiment is a key stage in creative thinking. Every new invention builds on a history of failed attempts. Resist pressure from friends, family, and professional contacts to do the next obvious thing (see Exercise 1.1 – Breaking out of default mode, p. 12). Every successful product brought to market required a thousand near misses. Experiment away. The most important work you will do on your career isn't about CV writing or interview preparation, it's about learning to think differently.

A surprising number of people say 'I'm not very creative'. Let's establish a ground rule. We're all creative – capable of inventing solutions to life's varied problems. Most problems are everyday: taking children in opposite directions in one car, paying this week's bills with next week's money, or mending using old bits and pieces rather than buying an expensive component. Sometimes it's a task we take for granted, such as taking an engine apart and putting it back together, perfectly, without a diagram, or caring for three or four difficult children at their most unpleasant, or making dinner out of six things in the cupboard. We are all creative. We have to be: that's how humans have survived.

### Shift your language

Try a change of vocabulary. Practise a register shift, from no to **yes**.

| The language of NO | The language of YES |
| --- | --- |
| It'll never work | Let's look at our alternatives |
| It's how I am; I was born that way | I can try a different approach |
| She makes me behave like that | I control my own feelings |
| It's against the rules | I'll invent a new rulebook |
| It's not for me | I need to find out more |
| I'm forced to | I will choose |

| In the real world . . . | I make my world real by . . . |
| Another mistake . . . | How interesting . . . |
| If only . . . | Let's try . . . |
| Never | It's all experimental |

'Whether you think you can or you can't, you're right.'

**Henry Ford**

### Distinguish between goals and dreams

We're all great at having 'safe' dreams: ideas we like to play with, assured that we will never have to do anything about them. They are daydreams that keep us warm on cold winter evenings. Goals are things we can do something about.

In his book *The Seven Habits of Highly Effective People*, Stephen Covey advises us to 'begin with the end in mind'. Many people believe that all you need to make the future happen is to set long-term objectives and stick to them with fanatical commitment. In *59 Seconds*, Richard Wiseman debunks a great deal of the theory of goal-setting. Wiseman demonstrates that it's a myth that writing down life-changing goals has a recordable effect. However, there is evidence to suggest that commitment to short-term goals is effective. If you break tasks down into mini-objectives and reward yourself for achieving them, you're more likely to make progress. Real goals require a first, second, and third step.

However, don't lose sight of the original dream. We're all more likely to move towards goals which energise and inspire.

### Feed your curiosity

Can people reinvent themselves? Some of us have no choice. In a rapidly changing world, we may need to do this more than once. Reshaping your career requires open-ended thinking, remaining curious and driven by your imagination. Learn how to cultivate tentative ideas rather than trash them. It's no use thinking 'I wonder about medicine . . .' if you immediately say 'Do I want to be a doctor or don't I?' Forcing a decision too early simply crushes creative thinking. Maybe not a doctor – maybe a medical journalist, a pharmacist, a nutritionist or a physiotherapist?

### *Make it so*

Do it as if all jobs pay the same. Do it as if all doors will open for you. Do it as if you were doing it for somebody else. Imagine a friend offers you a thousand pounds to find her ideal career path. If you took the task on, you wouldn't go back every five minutes saying 'you wouldn't like this', yet this is what we do for ourselves. If you were doing it for someone else, you'd keep looking for variations and angles, keep turning up new connections. Start by simply generating ideas for roles and sectors worth investigating. Look for things that tickle your curiosity, areas you find you talk about with enthusiasm – these are big clues to your future.

In *Star Trek: The Next Generation*, Captain Jean-Luc Picard (played by the inimitable Patrick Stewart) executed commands with three plain words: *Make it so*. There comes a point when it's healthy to move on from 'what if' to 'how could I make this work?' Think in terms of pilot schemes and experiments – low-risk ways of getting things moving. Extend yourself by studying in your own time. Take up voluntary activity outside work in order to experiment with your career longings. Short-term or temporary employment can sometimes help to provide a useful 'laboratory' for your career plans. Sometimes the best prompt for everyday experiment is: 'Don't think, just leap.'

### Ruts and channels

One of the reasons people don't think about finding enjoyable work is that human beings are adaptable. We can live in climates ranging from sub zero Arctic to sweltering heat. We can survive in the most demanding, unhealthy, and difficult conditions, and families can work, raise children, and live good lives even under the most brutal political regimes. Perhaps because of this built-in survival instinct, some of us have the capacity to do something that modern society finds odd and most of history saw as the norm. We can hold down an uninspiring job for decades. Given a world of choice, the fact that we can doesn't mean that we should.

People often say they are stuck in a career rut. The worst kind of rut is the *velvet rut*: you hate being in it, but it's just too comfortable to climb out of. Ruts stay ruts because you're stuck in your thinking. You know that something needs to change, but what? What's needed is breakthrough thinking, a great idea to move you forward. What you're probably going to need is to think a little differently, and behave a little differently.

Define the problem you'd like to solve in terms of a future emotional state. How would you like to feel in a year's time? What changes in you would others notice? What first step can you take tomorrow to make that change a possibility?

Many years ago I heard a motivational speaker in San Francisco deliver a great one-liner. I've tried to track down the name of the speaker, but without success, but I thank him anyway. He said: 'If you only live half your life, the other half will haunt you forever.'

## Behaviour and belief

The greatest barriers between you and an inspired career are not in the marketplace or on your CV, but in your mind.

Rule 1: we know that **behaviour follows belief**. If you believe evidence of your own ability, you are more likely to talk about your strengths credibly. If you feel confident and in control, that's how you'll act. So, believe in what you can do. Learn to accept your brain's own ability to create ideas, possibilities, connections, and to put thinking into practice.

It's often said that the creative mind can hold contradictory ideas at the same time. So to Rule 2: **belief follows behaviour**. In other words, acting out a part makes us think differently, and *it's easier to act your way into a new way of thinking than to think your way into a new way of acting.*

Try it. Behave as if you are already successful. For example, if you have to make a public presentation, then decide to act, walk, and talk as if you already have the full attention of your audience. Sit down for a job interview as if you're already working successfully in the role. Walk the walk, talk the talk, and something happens – you physically act your way into a new way of looking at yourself. That's why it's easier to have authority if you are dressed professionally, and why people are more assertive on the phone when they stand up. If you act confident or proficient, you become it – quicker than you imagine.

'We do not think ourselves into new ways of living, we live ourselves into new ways of thinking.' **Richard Rohr**

### Stop looking for negative reinforcement

There are more varieties of jobs out there than ever before, yet we still generally let our careers be shaped by accident, or accept second or third best because it's easier to stand still than to move forward. Most importantly of all, we insist on using the most limited kind of straight-line thinking in career planning and job search. Why? Essentially, we like to do what feels safe, even if that means being unhappy. There's a powerful part of the brain that says: *Stop here.*

*It's dull, but it's comfortable. Out there looks difficult and strange.*

And then you find evidence to support your position. You focus on stories of people of your age and background who tried to make a change and failed. I have a theory. At times when change threatens, we develop a personal radar that scans the horizon for information. Radar, as you know, is hungry for enemy objects. And we find them. You suddenly discover people who were made redundant and never found a job again. People beat a path to your door to tell you, *Don't do it . . . it will all come to tears.*

We come up with all kinds of negative messages to act as blocks to growth and change. If you believe you're 'not an ideas person' or 'not a leader', your brain is capable of making sure this becomes a self-fulfilling prophecy. If a golfer says, 'I bet I slice this ball', she probably will.

I'm indebted to Marie Brett, who told a story at one of our masterclasses for career coaches. She overheard two women on a bus in Northumberland talking about one of their daughters. 'These days', one explained, 'it's not about what you *want* to do, it's about what you *can* do'. Marie could hear the poor daughter's career derailed in one sentence. Another coach, Esi Kpeglo, talked about trying to reposition herself mid-life, building on her professional background. An elderly relative suggested, with real kindness, that it might be time to find a 'humbler' job like being a pot washer or postal worker. Other people shape our career thinking, and can easily reinforce a negative picture of the world.

### Focus on what's working, not on what isn't

Trainee airline pilots are taught, in an emergency, not to focus on what parts of the aeroplane aren't functioning. Instead they ask themselves, 'What do I have left working which will get me safely on the ground?' In the same way, we need to learn to put our attention on everything we're doing which is working – and what we have in our toolkit that can be used. Otherwise, it's easy to spend all your time and energy focusing on conversations that haven't worked, applications that fell at the first hurdle, or people who won't return your call. Everyone gets knock-backs. If you are the kind of person who takes rejection personally, don't beat yourself up about it – recruit some support.

'Action may not always bring happiness, but there is no happiness without action.' **William James**

### Go with the flow

Psychologist Mihaly Csikszentmihalyi coined the term 'flow' to describe a particular mental state where people feel engaged, absorbed, and purposeful. We are in 'flow' when time seems to pass quickly – often you forget to take meal breaks because you are 'into' something. Sometimes we experience this in simple but absorbing tasks like painting a wall, completing a jigsaw puzzle, or entering figures onto a spreadsheet. Sometimes the task is more complex and happens over a longer time frame. Remember times you felt like this and record them as evidence of motivated skills (see Chapter 7).

The fashion designer Ozwald Boateng was interviewed on BBC Radio 4 in March 2012. He mentioned that his father's career advice was 'if something comes easy to you, stick at it'. So he did, switching from a course in computer studies to fashion. His father quickly said that this wasn't what he had in mind, but Boateng stuck at it and has built a highly successful business with an international reputation. Your talents are not always evident until you discover them, but if you find something you do well that 'comes easy', it's a great place to start.

## Exercise 5.1 – Idea Grid

Once you have generated a number of tentative career ideas, you'll need to find some way of focusing on those that will really work for you.

1. Use blank cards or Post-it® notes to record goals. Don't exclude anything because it seems unrealistic.
2. Sort your cards into columns. Give each column a heading (for example, Professional, Learning, Financial, Personal).
3. Rank the columns. Place the most important column on the left, the least important on the right:

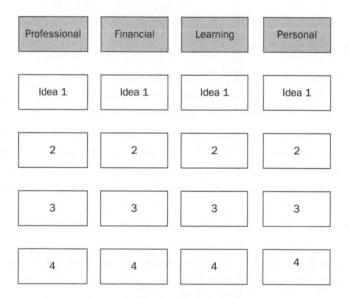

1. You might want to exclude ideas that you can't begin to address within a set period of time; for example, discard ideas you can't begin to work on within two years. So, 'Find time to write my novel' might have to go on the back burner for a year or two. It's up to you.

2. Put the ideas in rank order within each column, with the most important at the top.

Now stand back and look at your results. Better still, go away and do something else for an hour, then come back and look. What you have is a draft *prioritised* grid, with the most important, critical or immediately relevant ideas in the top left-hand corner.

You can use the same technique to come up with ideas to solve a problem. For instance, if your problem is 'How can I change my career without going back to full-time study?', you can come up with a range of potential ideas and solutions, without self-criticism or feeling forced into a decision too soon. Reward yourself for off-the-wall ideas. Sort, re-sort, reflect.

## Exercise 5.2 – Work themes

Starting from the inside means putting together a starting recipe for the kind of job that will work for you. One simple index of whether the job will work well for you is to think about the big themes that characterise work.

**Scoring:** Give each work theme a score between 1 and 5, where 1 = little interest, 3 = moderate interest, 5 = high interest.

| Creativity | Your preferred work is mainly about working imaginatively with ideas or designs; for example, the arts, performing, creative writing, visual design, lateral thinking, business creativity, adapting ideas, coming up with new ideas, challenging assumptions. |
|---|---|
| Score: | |

| Hands on | Your preference is working hands on, engaging with the physical world; for example, building, shaping, cooking, craft, DIY, working with animals, plants, machines, vehicles, sports, physical fitness, physiotherapy, or working outdoors. |
|---|---|
| Score: | |

| **Influence** | Your preference is working with and through other people and will involve: leadership, management, changing organisations, setting up a new business or department, inventing, reorganising, shaping teams, driving others, influencing, persuading, motivating, selling, getting results. |
| --- | --- |
| Score: | |

| **Information** | Your ideal work is mainly about working with information; for example, analysing, cataloguing, gathering, planning, managing projects, researching, tracking down information, working with numbers or accounts, making the most of computers. |
| --- | --- |
| Score: | |

| **Systems** | You are most attracted to working with systems; for example, processes, quality control, continuous improvement, legal processes, procedures, bookkeeping, record-keeping, database management, health and safety. |
| --- | --- |
| Score: | |

| **People** | Your preference is for working with people; for example, training, teaching, coaching, mentoring, developing, caring, nursing, nurturing, healing. |
| --- | --- |
| Score: | |

Look at your top three work themes. How is your career a unique interaction between these themes? How can you make sure that your work feeds all three? For example, if your top three work themes in order are Creativity, People, and Hands on, you'll want to ensure that your work allows you a high degree of creativity generated by teams of people, with the chance to invent new rules from time to time, but you'll be happiest working where you achieve results that you can see and feel. Remember, your work theme combination is a combination unique to you, because it also draws upon your knowledge, values, and experience.

## 'Must do' list

- ✓ Practise using different modes of thinking. Try a range of techniques for idea-generation and problem-solving (start by using them on everyday problems and then adapt them to career planning).
- ✓ Take dreams seriously, and see which ones will translate into goals. Write them down, somewhere, and tell someone you've done it.
- ✓ Record times when you were totally absorbed in tasks – either in work or outside it. What were you doing? What kind of roles involve tasks of this kind?
- ✓ Write a Plan A for the next 12 months. Things to include: first steps on the journey, measurable goals, the critical steps you need to follow to make things happen (writing articles, going to conferences, talking to people, getting your CV rewritten, finishing that book . . .).
- ✓ Look at your top three work themes. If you combine those three together, what ideas can you come up with?

**6**

# Your career drivers

'In order that people may be happy in their work, these three things are needed: They must be fit for it. They must not do too much of it. And they must have a sense of success in it.'

**John Ruskin**

*This chapter offers opportunities to:*

- Look at workplace turn-offs
- Think about the part money plays in your career
- Identify what motivates you
- Discover your career hot buttons.

## Turn-offs in the workplace

Go back to 'The good, the bad, and the just plain awful' on p. 31. Think about your hate list: the ten things you would like to change most (about the work you do, or the way you are at work). Write them down.

You might find it helpful to categorise some of your dissatisfactions: physical work environment, location, colleagues you work with, management style, status, recognition, people, tasks, variety, values of the organisation, and so on. Make sure you have recorded all the things that demotivate or irritate you.

What recruiters know is that everyone has career hot buttons – the things that keep us motivated in the long term.

Not everyone is good at identifying them. If you're asked why you want to leave a job, you use shorthand: 'The job stinks', 'The money's rotten', 'It's the way they treat you'. Build on that experience by asking 'What parts of the job felt boring or dispiriting?'

Now look at the flip side, the positive. What parts of the job encouraged you to head into work on a cold Monday morning? What parts of a job keep you interested, excited, focused?

## What *really* motivates you?

Recruiters will tell you that most often the first answer to this question is 'money'. The reason is that it's easy, convenient shorthand. In my interview training programmes, I pushed interviewers to probe to the next level. You may not be motivated by money at all, in fact. Throwing money at a problem does not make satisfied workers. Once money issues are resolved, deeper motivators kick in, such as being respected for what you know, seeing the job through to the finish, variety, making a difference, learning and work–life balance.

### 'I need the money'

Although everyone talks about money, it's is rarely the primary motivator in changing jobs. Sometimes workers take a pay cut for the right role. For a small proportion of people, earning at a high level is like an internal game. Most people want to feel moderately well paid.

Psychologists tell us that we are more influenced by loss than gain. If you lose a £5 note from your pocket, that might ruin you day, but finding £10 in the street may only cheer you up momentarily. A pay rise makes us feel good for a while, but the effect is short-lived. Employers recognise that high pay helps to keep workers, but doesn't necessarily make them more productive. Most people admit that if they get a new year pay rise it has an effect on their work performance for less than a month. However, if they receive a pay cut, it bothers them every time they see a pay slip, read a job advertisement, and every time they wonder what their friends are earning. Feeling underpaid, especially where you feel your work is not appreciated, has a long-term demotivating effect.

How do you have any sense of what you are worth? I have known individuals being interviewed for £40,000 and £80,000 jobs in the same week, with little real difference in responsibility or complexity. Markets often do very odd things with salaries. Have you ever calculated what you really cost your employer, including overheads, and then calculated what value you add to the bottom line, whether actual in terms of profits or metaphorically in terms of your invisible contribution?

'You ask what is the proper limit to a person's wealth? First, having what is essential, and second, having what is enough.'   **Seneca**

When asked 'How much money do you need to feel that you have enough?', I'm told that most people name a figure which is double their present income, whether they earn £15,000 or £150,000 a year. However, most careers books ask you to work out the minimum you need to pay all your bills and to eat. Unfortunately, far too many people confuse this figure with what they are worth.

Write down a figure in answer to each question below:

---

**What do you need to earn each month?**

When you have added up all your monthly bills, travel, insurance, health, and food costs:

**What do you need to live on?**      £ ☐

---

What would you need to earn to be relaxed about what you spend each month?

**What would be ENOUGH?**  £ [            ]

How do you value your skills, knowledge, and commitment? What do people with your skills and experience earn in your sector? If you know the earnings range, what do you have to do to be in the top 25%? Write an annual figure here.

**What are you worth?**  £ [            ]

Now think ahead. Assuming you keep motivated, keep learning, and move forward in your career:

**What annual earnings do you want to achieve in five years' time?**  £ [            ]

Some people overestimate their earning power, but this usually means they have not put enough work into matching their strengths against actual market opportunities. You know that goals are best achieved through small steps (see Chapter 5), so what are you going to do next? What can you do today to discover your market value? What first step will move you towards an interesting *and* relatively well-paid job?

## Exercise 6.1 – The 3-Minute Motivation Checklist

### What motivates you to get up in the morning and go to work?

You have £20 to spend on yourself. Spend it in the table below on the things that really motivate you in work. You might spend £20 on one item, or spread your money around (don't use units smaller than £1).

| | **Motivating factor** | **£££s** |
|---|---|---|
| 1 | **Status**<br>My worth is recognised in my job title/pay level/car/responsibilities . . . | |
| 2 | **Recognition**<br>I am recognised for my skills and contribution | |
| 3 | **Feedback**<br>I know when I am doing a good job | |
| 4 | **Skills balance**<br>My opportunities and skills are well matched | |
| 5 | **Challenge**<br>I like to take on new projects and problems | |
| 6 | **Success**<br>I enjoy being a winner | |
| 7 | **Personal development**<br>I have continuing opportunities to learn and stretch myself | |
| 8 | **Variety**<br>My work is varied and interesting | |
| 9 | **Responsibility**<br>I am responsible for important things/people/projects | |
| 10 | **Company values**<br>I recognise and agree with the values of my employer | |
| 11 | **Independence/freedom**<br>I have some control over how I spend my time at work and where I go | |
| 12 | **Expert**<br>I offer a valued, specialised contribution | |
| 13 | **Team membership**<br>I enjoy being part of an active, supportive team | |

| 14 | ***Making a difference contributing***<br>I can see what my contribution adds to the whole process | |
|----|----|----|
| 15 | ***Helping others***<br>My work contributes to others, or to society as a whole | |
| 16 | ***Meaning and fulfilment***<br>I find my work meaningful and fulfilling | |
| 17 | ***Security***<br>Knowing what I will be doing and earning in a year's time matters to me | |
| 18 | ***Earnings now***<br>I am relatively well paid compared with my peers | |
| 19 | ***Earnings potential***<br>My earnings will probably increase significantly in the future | |
| 20 | ***Fringe benefits***<br>The job has interesting perks | |

## Building on the 3-Minute Motivation Checklist

Review the motivators you have chosen. How different is this list from the way you would have completed it five or ten years ago? Motivators often change a great deal.

This exercise has been used more than any other in this book – with thousands of clients, workshop and conference delegates. Feedback reveals different ways it helps people making a career change:

1. Compare your scores with the job you're in at the moment. What drivers are missing from your current role? What difference would it make to you if more of them were present?
2. You can use it as a checklist of the ingredients you'd prefer to have in your next role (you won't get them all – see the 70% overlap on p. 49).

3. Look at where you have allocated £2 or more. Think about a time in work when that motivator was matched. Find someone to talk to about that experience. Make it one of the energised stories you prepare for interviews.

# Exercise 6.2 – Career hot buttons

Read all the questions below and then circle the overall score you feel is right in each category. Use the full scale rather than bunch all your scores in the middle.

| 1. Financial rewards |
|---|
| • How important is the money? How much re-energised would you be if your salary increased by 10%? 20%? How long would that feeling last? <br> • How motivated are you by financial rewards such as bonus payments? <br> • If you could do more of the interesting things in your job and fewer of the dull things, would you be just as happy with less money? <br> • When you're at a party and listening to people talk about their jobs, how much do you think about what they earn? How much does it matter to you if you're earning less than other people whose skills are no better than yours? |

**Financial rewards are:**

| 1 | 2 | 3 | 4 | 5 | 6 | 7 | 8 | 9 | 10 |
|---|---|---|---|---|---|---|---|---|---|
| Unimportant | | | Moderately important | | | | Very important | | |

| 2. Influence |
|---|
| • How much do you enjoy leadership and persuasion (high influence)? <br> • How much control do you like to have over people, situations, problems? <br> • How much does it trouble you when you have little influence over decisions? |

- Do you prefer to be in charge (high influence) or are you happy to follow a good leader (low influence)?
- How much do you like to have a say in change?

**Influence is:**

| 1 | 2 | 3 | 4 | 5 | 6 | 7 | 8 | 9 | 10 |
|---|---|---|---|---|---|---|---|---|----|
| Unimportant | | | Moderately important | | | | Very important | | |

### 3. Expertise

- How important is the feeling of being knowledgeable, skilled, expert?
- Are you generally happy knowing a lot about one focused area of knowledge?
- Do you enjoy a reputation as a specialist (high expertise) or are you flexible enough to take on a wide range of tasks (low expertise)?
- Do you enjoy it when others seek you out to ask for your advice or specialist knowledge?

**Having expertise is:**

| 1 | 2 | 3 | 4 | 5 | 6 | 7 | 8 | 9 | 10 |
|---|---|---|---|---|---|---|---|---|----|
| Unimportant | | | Moderately important | | | | Very important | | |

### 4. Independence

- How far do you prefer a mentor to a supervisor?
- Are you a self-starter? How much do you like to set your own deadlines?
- How much control do you like over how you will allocate your time in achieving a task?
- How important is it to you that you can decide how you spend your time?
- Do you like to have control over what you do (high independence) or are you happy to accept intelligent supervision (mid to low independence)?

**Independence at work is:**

| 1 | 2 | 3 | 4 | 5 | 6 | 7 | 8 | 9 | 10 |
|---|---|---|---|---|---|---|---|---|----|
| Unimportant | | | Moderately important | | | | Very important | | |

### 5. Relationships

- How important to you are close relationships at work?
- Do you intend to make friends through work?
- Are you more productive working in a team (high relationships) or quietly on your own (low relationships)?
- How important is it you to trust and be trusted?

**Relationships at work are:**

| 1 | 2 | 3 | 4 | 5 | 6 | 7 | 8 | 9 | 10 |
|---|---|---|---|---|---|---|---|---|----|
| Unimportant | | | Moderately important | | | | Very important | | |

### 6. Security

- How financially secure do you need to feel?
- How much does it matter that you have a nest egg, a safety net – a cushion against ill fortune (high security)?
- How happy are you to take on risks of various kinds (low security)?
- How important is it to know what you will be doing next year?

**Security in work is:**

| 1 | 2 | 3 | 4 | 5 | 6 | 7 | 8 | 9 | 10 |
|---|---|---|---|---|---|---|---|---|----|
| Unimportant | | | Moderately important | | | | Very important | | |

### 7. Status

- How much does your reputation matter to you?
- How important is it to you to have your skills recognised by your colleagues, your profession, your community (high status)?
- How far are you happy to work in the background , getting the job done, not minding who gets the credit (low status)?
- How important is it to you to have a job title that reflects the level and impact of your job?

**Status is:**

| 1 | 2 | 3 | 4 | 5 | 6 | 7 | 8 | 9 | 10 |
|---|---|---|---|---|---|---|---|---|----|
| Unimportant | | | Moderately important | | | | Very important | | |

### 8. Meaning and fulfilment

- How strongly do you feel about the value your work adds to your community or society at large?
- How aware are you of the damage your work might be doing to others, or to the environment?
- Do you hear yourself saying that your work should be *meaningful*?
- Are you happy to seek meaning outside your working life?

**My search for meaning through work is:**

| 1 | 2 | 3 | 4 | 5 | 6 | 7 | 8 | 9 | 10 |
|---|---|---|---|---|---|---|---|---|---|
| Unimportant | | | Moderately important | | | | Very important | | |

### 9. Imagination

- How much do you enjoy coming up with ideas or new ways of doing things?
- Do you prefer to let others come up with ideas while you do the detailed planning?
- Do you prefer to follow a system or set of rules (low imagination)?
- Or do you like to come up with new solutions to problems (high imagination)?

**Using imagination at work is:**

| 1 | 2 | 3 | 4 | 5 | 6 | 7 | 8 | 9 | 10 |
|---|---|---|---|---|---|---|---|---|---|
| Unimportant | | | Moderately important | | | | Very important | | |

Transfer your scores below:

| Career hot buttons – results | |
|---|---|
| *Career hot button* | **Score** |
| 1. Financial rewards | |
| 2. Influence | |
| 3. Expertise | |

| | |
|---|---|
| 4. Independence | |
| 5. Relationships | |
| 6. Security | |
| 7. Status | |
| 8. Meaning and fulfilment | |
| 9. Imagination | |

Now list your top 4 hot buttons below, in rank order. This may be straightforward, but you may find you have items with the same score. If so, make a decision about what matters most in a job. (For example, if your scores for **Influence** and **Status** are the same, ask yourself: 'Would I prefer a job where influence is *marginally* more important than status?')

| **My top 4 Career hot buttons** |
|---|
| 1. |
| 2. |
| 3. |
| 4. |

## *Building on the career hot buttons*

Look at your top four buttons, and think about your present or most recent role. How many of these drivers does the role satisfy? What's missing? What can you add to your present job, or seek in your next post?

(Occupational psychologist Stuart Robertson built on these career hot buttons when designing his very interesting Career Motivation Indicator. See www.careermotivation.co.uk)

## 'Must do' list

- ✓ What do you find unstimulating, unacceptable, and demotivating?
- ✓ When have you felt really motivated? Think of concrete examples: projects, occasions, teams.
- ✓ What blend of job ingredients might keep you motivated in the long term?
- ✓ What kind of role would match your top career hot buttons?
- ✓ How can you identify roles which are a better match for your career drivers?

# Celebrating your skills

'When love and skill work together, expect a masterpiece.' **Charles Reade**

*This chapter helps you to:*

- Map your hidden skills – the parts of your experience you take for granted
- Understand and communicate your motivated skills
- Communicate your skill set to your colleagues, managers, and potential employers
- Express skills and achievements as mini-narratives.

## Rediscovering your skills

Since you use and observe skills every day, you may think you're good at identifying them. Only a few people have both identified their skills and know how to talk about them. When asked 'what are your skills?', some people look blank, some list the skills they are currently using at work. At interview most people list *skills they believe they should talk about*. Your friends may identify and affirm skills they see you use, but they won't necessarily see all your skills or the things you enjoy doing most. If you want to make sure you never get a great career, one of the best strategies is never to reveal your full set of gifts. If you're determined to continue doing work that fails to stretch you or match your aspirations, that will do the trick.

**Example:** Bill uses his computer every day, but his real interest is natural history. He gives time freely to his local school, which asks him to come in to fix computer problems or advise on software. If he is invited to do anything with the children, it usually involves explaining something about computers. He's great at it: probably the best person the school can find. But what he really wants to do is to talk to the kids about pond life.

## Exercise 7.1 – Skills catalogue in nine steps

Take a pad of paper. List your skills in the ten steps below. Make sure you write down *skills* (for example, organising, planning, negotiating), not aspects of personality (for example, enthusiastic, reliable, calm).

1. Imagine it's Sunday night and you are looking forward to activities and projects in the week ahead. What do you see yourself doing?
2. Imagine you're having a brilliant day at work. If someone was following you round with a video camera, what activities would the recording show?
3. Think of the most enjoyable job you've ever done. What skills were you using?
4. Think of a project you look back on with pride. What skills were you using?
5. Think about a time when you surprised yourself by doing something you didn't know you were capable of doing. What was the skill you used?
6. Think about times when you have received praise for your work performance. What skills were mentioned?
7. Write down any other skills you are good at *and* you enjoy using.
8. Look at all the skills you have recorded in steps 1–7. If you could choose only one skill from this list, which one energises you most?

9. Finally, think about a day at work when you were entirely absorbed in what you were doing, time passed quickly, and you went home feeling a 'buzz'. Find someone to talk to about that day, and ask them to make a list, while you are talking about all the skills you were using. Add any new skills to your list.

When you have completed Exercise 7.1, you should have a fairly comprehensive list of your main skills. This list should provide a useful mix of the skills you have noticed and those which have been valued by others. If you want to cross-check this list or find better phrases to describe your skills, try the **JLA Skill Cards** (see p. 99).

Now you have a good basic list of the skills you have, you might find it helpful to see how these skills fit into different **skill categories,** for example:

- Skills connected with **information** (research, data, analysis).
- Skills connected with **imagination** (creating, designing, building).
- Skills connected with **planning** and **systems** (structures, processes, organisation).
- Skills connected with **growth** and **enterprise** (making new things happen, being an entrepreneur).
- Skills connected with **influencing people** (leading, driving change, managing stakeholders).
- Skills connected with **developing people** (coaching, training, mentoring).

## Unwrap your gifts

Few of us see what a well-equipped skills toolbox we've been given. We use skills without recognising or crediting them, and we fail to bring out our latent talents, blinking, into the light. You have been given a unique set of talents. Unique not because of one, primary, virtuoso skill that commends you to the world, but because of the way all your skills are uniquely combined in you. Unique because you are the only person with your skills, exercised through your personality, your history, your viewpoint. No one else can be you, in your particular situation in life. You can always find somebody who can employ a particular skill better than you, but they can't *be you.*

However, be careful how you think about *transferable* skills. A lot of people assume that they only need to mention their skills and an enlightened employer will see how they are relevant to the role on offer. In practice, you are likely to be excluded from any selection process early if you don't describe your experience in terms that are immediately meaningful to an employer. Skills don't transfer on their own – you have to explain how what you have done is relevant.

Employers see many candidates who claim to be skilled but fail to provide supporting evidence – for example, *I am a good communicator.* What kind of communication? What do you mean by good? Say something about the level of your skills and about the context: *I regularly communicated difficult messages to team members, keeping them informed and motivated – resulting in improved staff retention over a three-year period of organisational change.*

## The skills below your radar

Some of us have skills we can describe well, but there are huge areas of unmapped territory. How many of your skills fit one of the following categories?

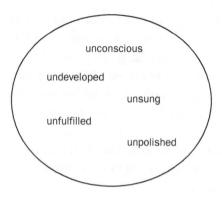

### Unconscious skills

Unconscious skills are the skills you use so frequently they have become invisible to you. I sometimes call them 'wallpaper skills'. When you put up new wallpaper you're very aware of it for a month or so, and then you gradually stop noticing it once you get used to it. It springs back into focus when someone walks into your home and says nice things about the way you have redecorated. Therefore, you notice your 'wallpaper' skills when others see them. It's generally useful for people to remind you what you're good at, but especially so when they spot skills you no longer see.

**Example:** Maureen's great skill is untangling messy personal situations. She works quietly in the background, helping people to see things clearly, encouraging the parties to put anger aside and seek common ground. Others see her do it: it's oiling the wheels, building community. She was entirely unaware that she has these skills until a friend said, 'Do you know what you do most of the time? You're the cement between the bricks of our community.' She never gets the opportunity to use these skills at work, so she says nothing about them in her CV.

**Example:** Norma can't walk past a piece of fabric without touching it. She has a good eye for texture, colour, and pattern, and for matching materials simply and cheaply to make a room look great. She has a knack of walking into a room and knowing how to make it look more welcoming, more 'together' by making a few simple changes. Last year her friend brought out these 'wallpaper' skills and found a set of undeveloped and marketable skills underneath – becoming a 'house doctor', helping other people to sell their homes quickly by reading the mind of the buyer and offering a series of low-cost, high-imagination solutions to make a home look great and sell quickly.

Sometimes these are skills you use only occasionally, perhaps under pressure or in special moments. You often don't notice yourself exercising these skills in the heat of the moment, or you don't claim ownership: things just happen. In an emergency, for example, there is often someone present who has great clarity of mind, organising people, calling an ambulance and preventing panic.

### Undeveloped skills

We're often very good at talking about the skills we lack, or the skills we feel are not up to scratch. You might gain more by focusing on skills that you have never really had the opportunity to develop, skills you instinctively feel you might be good at if you only had the chance.

How do you know they are there? Think about the skills you admire in others, or times when you have watched someone at work and thought 'I wouldn't mind having a go at that . . .'. Sometimes curiosity can quickly lead to new skills. Stretch yourself. Have a go.

**Example:** Nick is a keen photographer but a novice in terms of the digital age. He looked at the images produced by others but felt that he had no chance of equalling some of the work they did using expensive software. He decided to follow his curiosity, and asked some of his photographer friends to demonstrate the software they were using to process images from their digital cameras. His most important question each time was, 'how long did it take for you to learn this?' When he found entry-level software he liked, he bought it, catalogued all his photographs, and learned how to make basic images into great prints.

### Unsung skills

You know you possess these skills, are confident using them, but you feel that most employers would put no value on them. As a result, you don't talk about these skills or try to improve them.

**Example:** Sue's passion is ballroom dancing, but she leaves it off her CV because she feels it's irrelevant to work. One day, she heard of a college lecturer who taught business skills through ballroom dancing. Formal dancing teaches timing, responsiveness, leading and following, reading signals, anticipating change, and paying attention to personal space. Sue realised that using these skills at work was what made her a brilliant PA.

We often think of skills like this as 'hobby skills'. They could include horticulture, craft skills, fine hand-to-eye coordination, being good at crosswords, being a great sports coach. Job-changers often say, 'I talk to my friends about this stuff all the time, but I don't know how to fit this kind of stuff into my CV or talk about it at interview.'

**Example:** Sally has held a number of voluntary positions, connected with school, church, and Scouting. In the past ten years she has acted as treasurer, leader, resource manager, transport coordinator, catering manager, and team leader.

She condenses this into a throwaway phrase on her CV: 'voluntary interests'.

This category often includes so-called 'soft' skills. Many have a skewed idea of the business world: hard skills are seen as relevant, soft skills as 'nice to have' or ten-a-penny. The paradox, of course, is that some of the most difficult tasks are achieved through well-crafted soft skills such as careful persuading, influencing, and negotiating. Yet many candidates are worried that their 'soft' skills don't have a place in today's workplace.

Look for those moments when you say 'things just happened . . . it all came together at the last minute'. Who made it come together? If it was you, how did you do it? The clue for a skill that has value is that something changed because of your involvement. Ask someone who saw the event what it was you did, and then think about how you can build on that experience. If the skill is valuable to you, reveal its value to others. Make better connections between the skills you love using outside work and what you do best 9 to 5.

### Unfulfilled skills

Your unfulfilled skills are the things you'd love to do. *Listen to those dreams calling you:* I always wanted to . . . paint watercolours, ride a horse, write my autobiography, run a soup kitchen, build my own house . . .

How do we turn these fantasy scenarios into real opportunities? Sometimes by not taking them exactly at face value, but by interrogating them for clues. If you've always fancied being a long-distance lorry driver, for example, this may be a specific calling or may be a strong indication that you like to have a great deal of freedom in your job. Sometimes the fantasy is a simple invitation. If you've always dreamed of being a novelist, take a writing class, write the opening paragraph, read more novels . . . do anything, but do something.

The real test of longing is that the idea won't leave you alone until you do something about it. The crunch comes when impulse needs to translate into action. Want to be prime minister? Join a political party, achieve some kind of elected office, take the first steps towards becoming an MP.

Watch for activities that quite literally fill your dreams. I sailed as a boy, not particularly well. I often dreamt about sailing again, and in the dream I usually felt I had no idea what I was doing. At the age of 40, I took up sailing again, and because I had practised sailing so often in my head, I was actually better at it. I've heard this phenomenon called 'learning to ski in the summer, learning to swim in the winter'. Sports research reveals that training by visualising events is almost as powerful as real experience. If that's true, then imagined skills are more powerful than you think.

Nothing is as damaging as a ruthless policy of ignoring your unfulfilled skills. Try a job on a short-term basis. Work for nothing just to get the feel of it. Shadow someone doing the job to find out if it's what you'd really like to do. Take a short course rather than a three-year degree.

'A new idea is delicate. It can be killed by a sneer or a yawn; it can be stabbed to death by a joke or worried to death by a frown on the right person's brow.'   **Charles Brower**

### Unpolished skills

Unpolished skills are skills you have identified, but you have settled for competence when you know you are capable of far more.

**Example:** Maya learned through her job in customer services to deal with complaints, and when to refer difficult calls to managers. She had learned the job inside out, but hated any change: new products, new support services. She had failed to stretch herself, to see what she was really capable of, because she had never looked at the underlying master skill: *keeping customers happy*. Once Maya learned to develop that skill, to invent new ways of helping people, she began to grow and was promoted to supervisor.

**Example:** When you learn to swim, you begin by thinking of it as organised movement. Somewhere, you think, there's a special combination of movements that will keep me above water and move me forward. The barely competent swimmer achieves that, and no more. *That'll do. I can swim.* Bill broke through that stage when he realised that swimming wasn't about movement or power, but a form of guided floating. With that idea in mind, he progressed to swimming several lengths. Then he discovered that it was also about timed breathing. Control the timing and breathing, and you can continue swimming just like you can continue walking. The first skill breakthrough will rarely be the last.

## What if I don't get much out of the skills I use?

Sometimes you get the biggest insights by spotting skills you're good at but don't enjoy using. If you are in demand for these skills, you may still be able to learn to love them, but you'll probably need to find ways of stretching yourself. People who dislike what they do have often hit a flat patch on their learning curve. If not, it could be that you feel the skill is not worth using – in which case look at the values exercises in Chapter 9.

Alternatively, say no to unfulfilling tasks more often, and negotiate opportunities to use skills you enjoy. If you really can't reshape your current job (don't give up at the first attempt), perhaps it's time to move on.

# Exercise 7.2 – Skill clips

If your life is a movie, when you talk about yourself in a job search you've got to decide on just a few frames. Movies are promoted through trailers – the whole plot condensed into two minutes. The **skill clips** exercise sends you back to the cutting room to create a condensed, all-action version of you.

In the movie of your life, what are the key moments? Your best action scenes are the ones where you're doing things, getting results, interacting with people, starting or finishing projects.

Home movie rules for editing and composing your skill clips include:

1. **Zoom in as tight as possible** – avoid long sequences. One day is good. One hour is better. Keep it concise. Like a movie clip, it's got to convey a lot in a short space of time.
2. **Use slow motion** – reveal the action as it happens by thinking about what you did and how you did it.
3. **Use a good screenplay** – does this scene convey a message about skills, about overcoming obstacles?
4. **Keep the star in shot** – make sure this scene is about the hero: you.
5. **Make sure the clip has a happy ending** – an achievement or a skill revelation.

Fix on one event. Start with an occasion when you felt a great sense of success or achievement. Picture your 'clip', and give it a title. Then ask yourself the following skill discovery questions:

| | |
|---|---|
| What obstacles did I have to overcome? | What did I have to do to achieve this? |
| What was the task or challenge? | How did I work with others? |
| What planning did I need to do? | What was my best moment? |
| What skills did I see myself use? | How did I surprise myself or others? |
| What skills did others see me use? | What did I do personally? |

Prompts for your skill clips include:

- Think of times when you achieved something you are proud of. This doesn't need to be a work-related achievement. How did you do it? What difference did you make? Turn the event over in your mind until you see skills, particularly those you don't normally claim for yourself.
- Now look at your achievements from your non-working life. Times in the past when you overcame the odds, did something that surprised you.
- Think about work-related clips that demonstrate the full range of skills: things, people, information, concepts, etc.

Keep drawing up these skill clips, either alone or, with a fellow career developer. If you show a series of movie clips from the work of famous film director Alfred Hitchcock, you see similarities of style and content. After five or six skill clips, you'll start to notice a pattern of skills, or a set of *master skills*, and you'll get a strong sense of what you are really good at *and* enjoy doing.

## Example skill clip

| TITLE: 'Top of the world' | | | |
|---|---|---|---|
| INTRODUCTION:<br>I've always been frightened of heights. I was pretty unfit. My work team challenged me to climb Cwm Clogwyn in Snowdonia. | | | |
| **[Scenes]**<br>**Opening shot:**<br>**The problem** | **First step** | **Main action** | **Ending** |
| Panic! Fear of failing. Sponsorship for a good cause convinced me to go ahead | Weighing up the problem. Deciding what I needed to learn and practise | Setting off – the real thing. Putting theory and training into practice. Scary! | I made it! Photograph at the summit. Elation |
| *Skills I used*<br>Recognising my limitations. Overcoming fear | *Skills I used*<br>Learning from friends, practising on a climbing wall. | *Skills I used*<br>Working as a team, learning to rely on others. | *Skills I used*<br>Celebrating – enjoying what we had achieved as |

| | Learning to climb and belay, understanding equipment. Risk management? Anticipating and measuring problems | Responding (fast!) to instructions. Helping others to cope with their fear. Keeping people's spirits up with humour! | a team, and my special role in our success. Reflecting on what I had managed by overcoming fear and relying on my colleagues. Insight: new ways of working together |
|---|---|---|---|

## *Express achievements as mini-narratives*

Communicate skills and linked achievements as concise stories (see 'Telling Tales' in Chapter 16). When you talk about your best skills, use the structure outlined below: outline the problem, talk briefly about what you did, and state the outcome.

| Story: Beginning | Middle | End |
|---|---|---|
| *The problem* | *What I did* | *The outcome* |
| My company needed to simplify its accounting system and save money | Identified, researched, and introduced an off-site central accounting function | 25% savings, and the new accounts centre came online to budget and on deadline |

## Exercise 7.3 – Motivated skills

What skills do you really enjoy using? Think about a time you were so engrossed in a task that you lost all track of time – moments when you felt completely yourself.

Look at skills you have identified in Exercise 7.1. Put them into a grid as below:

### *Your motivated skills*

|  | Skills I love using | Skills I quite enjoy using | Skills I don't enjoy using |
|---|---|---|---|
| Skills I perform well |  |  |  |
| Skills I perform reasonably well but need to develop |  |  |  |
| Skills I do not perform well |  |  |  |

Skills in the darker areas are those you should probably be using and developing. How many of these skills do you use in your current role?

## Exercise 7.4 – Skills circle

Go back to your list of skills from Exercise 7.1. Highlighter your top 12 skills and write them in a circle, like the 12 points of a clock, as in the **Skills Clock** below.

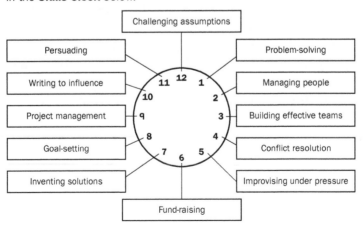

Try combining skills at different points of the clock face. Ask yourself, 'When have I used these two skills together? What sort of work would benefit from a combination of these two skills?' You might, for example, combine 2 *Managing people* and 7 *Inventing solutions*. This might mean: inventing new management systems, devising new ways of looking at management issues, such as giving people the tools to solve their own problems.

Combining 12 *Challenging assumptions* with 6 *Fund-raising* might make you think about turning the whole idea of fund-raising on its head. You might look at the question, 'How can we persuade more people to give us money?' and turn it around: 'How can we get people to persuade us to take their money?' Your fund-raising campaign may find a way of empowering people to select charities that exactly match their values.

## 'Must do' list

- ✓ Find the best way to discover your hidden skills. Enlist the help of a good listener, a patient friend or a professional career coach.
- ✓ Look at the connections between your dreams, your interests, and the skills you love using. There's a magic combination somewhere.
- ✓ Try at least four skill clips. Write out the skills you discover. Look at the skills that keep coming up time and again.
- ✓ Identify achievements for the different stages of your career.
- ✓ Practise talking about your skills in a way that sounds interesting rather than pushy.

**Further help to identify your skills and achievements**

The **JLA Skill Cards** give you an opportunity to identify and understand your top skills – not just the things you're good at, but the skills which give you most energy. Currently in its fourth edition, this card sort is popular with both job hunters and coaches. The cards allow you to choose from a comprehensive and up-to-date range of skills valued in today's workplace. Exercises are provided so you end up with a list of your motivated skills and linked achievement stories.

The **JLA Skill Cards** come with a full set of instructions and exercises to provide achievement evidence for your CV and job interviews, plus advice on communicating skill evidence to employers. See **www.johnleescareers. com** or search for 'JLA Skill Cards' on **Amazon.co.uk**.

For further tips on communicating your skills at interview, see *Knockout Interview* (McGraw-Hill, 2017).

# 8

# Your House of Knowledge

'My work is a game – a very serious game.'
**M.C. Escher**

*This chapter helps you to:*

- Tap your hidden knowledge
- Understand how your preferred interests provide huge clues about career satisfaction
- Make new connections between what you know and what you can do.

## What do you choose to know about?

Just as we all have hidden skills, we have concealed, but vital, areas of knowledge. What's powerful about your hidden knowledge is not just what you know, but why you know it. A certain amount of knowledge is imposed on us in school, but from the age of 14 or so we begin to make choices about our academic subjects. All the subjects we read, learn, and think about in our own time tell us a huge amount about our personality, aspirations, and interests.

Don't reject the possibility that there are new areas of knowledge you have yet to discover. One of the benefits of studying a wide range of subjects is students are exposed to areas of thinking that don't look interesting beforehand. It's one of the reasons why exercises focusing on skills and knowledge don't work very well with young people – they just haven't explored enough yet.

## Exercise 8.1 – House of Knowledge

This exercise helps you to identify the things you know about. It will help you to record interests that may provide links to potential work sectors. What you choose to learn about is a vital part of who you are.

What do you know about? In answering that question, people usually talk about expertise they use at work, or what they have studied. This is merely scratching the surface.

Look at the multi-storey house shown below. It has a ground floor, first floor, and second floor. It has an attic and a basement, and a garage at the side. Each level of that house represents areas of knowledge.

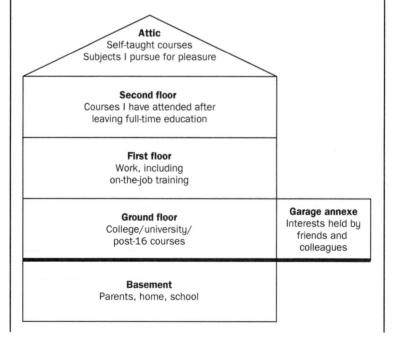

Like most exercises in this book, this works better if you have a conversation with someone while you are doing the exercise, or as soon as you have completed it.

1. Begin with the **basement** of your house, the firm foundations provided by your home and school. The following questions will help:
   - What did you learn from your parents? What was your favourite subject at school?
   - What projects or activities engaged you outside the classroom?
   - What was the first thing you wanted to read when you put aside your textbooks? What was that about?
   - When were you so enthusiastic about a subject at school or college that you went off and found more to read in your own time?
2. Complete the list for the **ground**, **first**, and **second floors**. Think of knowledge areas which do not yet appear in your CV – including the things you forgot you know about. Here are some prompts:
   - What training courses have you attended which you found stimulating? Think about (a) courses you chose to put yourself on and (b) courses you were sent on that turned out to be more interesting than you expected. What was the topic?
   - What subjects led you to turning points in your life (that night school in Photoshop that made you change degree course, for example)?
   - What subjects have you enjoyed training others in?
   - When in your career were you hungry to extend your learning?
3. Now think about your leisure activities and interests. This is your **attic**, the part of your brain where you store all that old junk you've forgotten you have, stuff you never thought you would find a use for. What areas of knowledge are hidden in those dusty trunks? Some prompts again:
   - When did you teach yourself something or learn something just for your own amusement?
   - When do you find yourself reading, talking or thinking about a subject and others have to shut you up? When do you find yourself so engrossed in an article or a book that the time passes unnoticed?
   - Given a free choice, what subjects would you choose to talk about over a relaxed meal?

- Think of a time when you have enjoyed learning about someone else's favourite subject or hobby. What was the subject?
- Which internet pages do you have bookmarked at home?
- If you could teach a workshop on any subject in the world, to any audience, and given unlimited preparation time, what would that subject be?
- If you could learn about any subject in the world, from any teacher, what would that subject be?
- If you were accidentally locked into a large bookshop for the weekend, in which section would you camp out? Once you got bored, where would you go next? And next? Write down the headings displayed on the bookshelves.
- When your Sunday newspaper arrives, fat with different sections, which part do you turn to first? Which part second?
- If you received a bequest from an aged relative that would fund a return to full-time education, what would you study?
- If you won the lottery and didn't have to work, you'd spend a year to two indulging yourself, but eventually you would get bored. What might you want to learn about to fill the time?

4. Last but not least, the **garage**. It's in an annex at the side because it's about vicarious interests, living life through the eyes and minds of other people. Think about close friends whose interests you share. My very dear friend Peter Maybank has a long-held interest in the First World War. I've joined him on battlefield trips to both Verdun and the Somme, and I realised through this experience how important the enthusiastic knowledge of others can be in shaping my own.

Look at your complete house. What have you missed out? It'll probably be things you consider 'trivial', such as cooking, home-making or family history. If you enjoy it, include it.

Try to remember what really interests you and all the things you have *chosen to know about*. This can trigger motivation to investigate new work sectors. The exercise also looks at knowledge you undervalue.

'The most successful people are those who do all year long what they would otherwise do in their summer vacation.'  **Mark Twain**

## The kind of knowledge that won't leave you in peace

The attic of the House of Knowledge potentially reveals more about us than any other part of the building. This is where we store away the special projects, the things that call to us from time to time and just won't go away.

I had the chance to work with the Liverpool-based photographer Colin McPherson some time back and asked him in passing, 'Do you still enjoy taking photographs when you're not taking them for a living?' He pulled out a card with one photograph on it, part of his long-term project documenting the last salmon net fishermen on the east coast of Scotland (see www.colinmcpherson.com).

Chapter 11 looks at how some people feel 'called' to certain roles. A very common piece of career advice is 'follow your passion' – suggesting you should build a career around your strongest interest. This often doesn't work. The website 80000hours.org looked at over 60 studies of what makes a 'dream job' and found that 'following your passion can lead you astray. Steve Jobs was passionate about Zen Buddhism before entering technology. Condoleezza Rice was a talented classical musician before she started studying politics. Rather, you can develop passion by doing work that you find enjoyable and meaningful.' The website argues that job satisfaction needs multiple ingredients: being engaged by varied and stimulating tasks; helping other people; using motivated skills; having supportive colleagues; being treated well by an organisation and avoiding major negatives such as job insecurity; and, finally, a role that fits your personal life. Focusing simply on 'following your passion' ignores one of this book's clearest statements: there are many elements in the deal.

However, this doesn't give you permission to ignore strong interests entirely. They may not map exactly onto your work role, but they provide important clues about potential sectors. For example, if your spare time joy is building boats, you may not want to do this for a living because it wouldn't pay enough and would ignore other skills. However, the amateur boat-builder might investigate options for working in craft-related sectors, construction, boat sales or supplies, or shipping (see Chapter 10 on identifying sectors).

## 'Must do' list

- ✓ Look at your completed House of Knowledge. What activities in your past filled you with energy? Where is that energy today?
- ✓ Sit with someone else while they explore their own House of Knowledge, and your partner's ideas will probably jog your memory.
- ✓ If you've caught yourself saying 'ah, I really used to enjoy . . .', then look at why you dropped the activity or interest. Is there a 'yes, but' in there somewhere?

# Personality fit

'If you are all wrapped up in yourself, you are
overdressed.' **Kate Halverson**

*This chapter helps you to:*

- See how personality and work are connected
- Identify your working style
- Spot contexts and roles where your personality fits
- Anticipate psychometric testing
- Gain insights into your values and how you apply them at work.

## Personality type

Personality type is broadly connected with career choice –
but the word *broadly* should be emphasised. If you're a
people person, you will almost certainly choose an occupation that allows you to work with others, but this could be in
a very wide range of work sectors. Equally, quiet people can
work for organisations which are full of outgoing people.
So, given the wide range of sectors you might work in with
any personality, it's perhaps best to focus on areas of comfort and discomfort.

### *Your personality in the workplace*

**Work role.** If the majority of the tasks you undertake are a good match to your temperament, work generally fits well. For example, if you love the opportunity to perform detailed work and that's exactly what you're hired to do, the working day may be well balanced. If you find yourself constantly outside your comfort zone, that's a fair indication that your personality doesn't suit your work.

Where your **values** are matched in work, you may feel you're doing something more meaningful, and your small part of the world is improved by the fact that you're doing it. Alternatively, if you feel there is something missing, it may be that your role is hollow: productive on the outside, but empty at its core (see Exercises 9.2 and 9.3 in this chapter).

Using the right **skills** can be related to personality. Doing things well and enjoying what you do may feed a sense of self-esteem. A mismatch between your motivated skills (see Chapter 7) and your work role can easily make you feel under-appreciated.

Your personality provides strong clues about the kind of **team** you would work best in. Look at past team experiences to work out what your natural role is in any team – Leader? Diplomat? Go-getter?

Personality also links strongly with the kind of **boss** you will work best with. How do you feel about being micro-managed? How important is it to have a boss who trusts you to get on with the job and supports you even if you make the odd mistake?

Do you respond best to a small **organisation** that offers variety and challenge or where you need to be self-reliant, or are you happier in the more defined structure of a larger organisation? Do you feel constrained by too small an organisation, or by being an anonymous cog in a large concern? Perhaps you have struck the wrong balance between growth and security, between variety and structure.

**Career drivers** also have strong links to personality (see Chapter 6 on your career hot buttons). Compare your main drivers to what your job requires of you. Look at past roles as well – how is your work performance changed by being in a role that more closely matches your hot buttons?

**Working conditions** can affect mood and commitment in some personality types. How far is your motivation affected by the following: location, travel, the kind of building you work in, what you can see from your office window, where you spend your lunch hour?

Self-esteem is often linked to **personal growth**, including the ability to keep learning. Does your job keep stretching you? What have you learned in the past 12 months? Who sets your learning agenda? For some personality types, growth is linked to **advancement**. Is your present role a useful stepping-stone to the future? Do you have a clear plan for the next five years? Do you need one? How would a recruiter see your present role: as a dead end, a side alley or a building block in your career?

People often seek different kinds of **pace** and **challenge** at work. Do you prefer to be constantly facing new problems, or do you need time to deal with the work you're given and to process new ideas? Does rapid change fill you with energy, or do you find it threatening? Does your organisation make things happen quickly enough for you? Are you being pushed to work at a speed that feels uncomfortable? How do you feel about leaving things half completed?

## Getting a handle on your personality

'To the man who only has a hammer in the toolkit, every problem looks like a nail.' **Abraham Maslow**

Exercise 9.1 offers some broad indicators about your personality. Put a score on each scale, avoiding the midpoint.

*Note*: there are no 'right' answers. Think about the way you see yourself, the way others see you, and the way you react under pressure. Increased self-awareness will provide good clues about your best fit in terms of people and organisational culture.

After completing the chart, ask someone who knows you well to judge how far you have produced an accurate self-portrait. Use this information to increase your level of awareness of the way your personality operates in work.

## Exercise 9.1 – Personality Overview

How would you describe yourself?

| Confident | Cautious |
|---|---|
| Head in the clouds | Practical |
| Abstract | Concrete |
| Logical | Intuitive |
| Emotional | Analytical |
| Optimistic | Pessimistic |
| Open to change | Reluctant to change |
| Self-reliant | Need the approval of others |
| Emotionally vulnerable | Self-assured |
| Follower | Leader |
| Solo artist | Team player |
| Steady | Flexible |

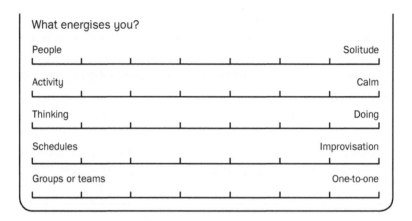

### Go with the grain

TV programmes about career change often show participants being encouraged to 'fake it' – to bluff, claiming skills and experience they don't possess. This has little connection with reality. Selection processes gather information carefully, scrutinising candidate backgrounds.

However, you might be tempted to fake or masks aspects of your personality. This is usually based on the assumption that only one personality style is acceptable. You'll hear people say, for example, 'I really need to be more assertive.' Similarly, people believe that they aren't smart enough to be offered a job. Intelligence is often considered just in terms of IQ scores, or success in passing examinations. Howard Gardner argued that intelligence has many forms. Some people are good with language, some with numbers, visual images, logic, music; others have highly developed physical skills and awareness. Others may have no qualifications but have practical common sense and problem-solving capacity. Some have highly developed 'people skills', others are better at tasks requiring quiet reflection. In other words, people are 'smart' in different kinds of ways.

Don't beat yourself up for not being someone else; recognise your strengths. Identify the contexts where you work at your best, and seek them out. It's like working with a piece of wood – life is much easier if you go with the grain. Stop believing you need to be someone else, and start celebrating the way *you* are. Of course, at interview, it's good to present the best version of *you* – what you are like on a good day.

## Personality – tests and questions

During an interview, you may face straight-on questioning about how closely you match the job, but also questions that seem to have very little connection to job content at all (see Chapter 16). Questions about personality can sound vague or off the wall, but what an employer is usually trying to do is to assess the human impact of giving you a job – how you will react to others around you, and how you will relate to the wider world, including customers. Team fit is also an important consideration.

Start by imagining what kind of personality will do well in the role. That's the picture you need to match. Think about whether your CV evidence and interview answers will confirm or undermine this picture. Show rather than tell – rather than make the empty claim 'I work well under pressure', give an example. Do the same thing for all the key personality characteristics you can spot on the employer's shopping list. Rehearse strong mini-narratives that convey useful all-round strengths like flexibility, working with difficult people, overcoming problems, or getting things done with thin resources.

There are a number of psychometric tests you may face. These vary from ability tests, including numerical and verbal reasoning tests, to personality tests. The Myers–Briggs Type Indicator (MBTI) is used widely in staff development, but has its critics because it is based on Jungian type theory. More recent tests (for example, OPQ and 16PF5) give results based on the 'big five' traits. Tests of this nature should be conducted by a qualified practitioner. (See the document *Psychological Testing: A test taker's guide* published by the British Psychological Society: ptc.bps.org.uk.)

Where you've undergone personality testing, you may be asked in more detail about your working style, particularly if the test results suggest that you might not be an ideal fit. Again, have some good examples up your sleeve and show that you're capable of adapting to a wide range of circumstances.

When going through a selection process, you may be asked to take a psychometric test of some kind. I couldn't think of anyone better than my colleague Peter Fennah, Chartered Psychologist, to explain the process:

---

**Personality tests – what to expect from an assessment process**

You will be asked to complete a personality questionnaire (untimed), typically completing it online before you attend the assessment centre. At the same time, you are likely to be asked to complete standard numerical, verbal, and abstract ability questions, though these would be under timed conditions of between 6 to 25 minutes each. There will be a couple of example questions to complete to ensure you fill the form in correctly (pay attention here if you know you get easily distracted). Ensure you are relaxed and distraction-free. Ideally, you should seek to complete each exercise in one sitting taking a break between activities – if you have to stop part way through or lose your internet connection, your answers are likely to have been saved up until this point, so you shouldn't lose more than a few answers and can pick it up again from where you left off.

For ability questionnaires, don't expect to answer the same questions as other candidates you know who have completed the same assessment. Test publishers draw on a large bank of questions and have automated systems to mix up the actual questions.

The reason you may be asked to complete a personality questionnaire as part of the recruitment process is to determine your likely fit for the role/team, your response to the pressures of performing the role, and operating within the culture of the organisation. At this point you may be thinking of how to skew your answers to match what the employer wants to hear. There are three risks to this. First, psychologists designing robust personality questionnaires include measures to check the consistency of your answers and compare them to other population groups. This reveals exaggerated responses which will be probed at interview. Being 'found out' in this way can be uncomfortable and unhealthy for your career. Second, if you are a poor fit for some parts of the role but your performance on the other elements of the assessment process is good, the employer would normally want to talk about effective coping strategies to help you perform to your best in the role. If you have skewed your answers, then this conversation has little value. Third, no one is a perfect match. Every person will shape the role around their strengths so it is better to be authentic, work with the way you are, and attempt to make a success of the role. If you really are a wrong match, then it is far better for both you and the employer to know this early; another role may be available that would suit you better.

Employers following best practice will provide you with detailed feedback on your psychometric results. This may partly be through a report document, but ideally you should also have around 30 minutes with a trained professional who will discuss your results and check that they have been interpreted accurately. Psychometric tools are not perfect and there can be a lot of legitimate reasons for different results to emerge. Therefore, if there are any surprises in the results, it is good to explore these. This is why trained professionals play a key role in the feedback and assessment process.

**Peter Fennah** is a Chartered and Registered Occupational Psychologist and accredited executive coach. He focuses upon developing agile leadership and aiding those in career transition. Visit www.careersynergy.com

## Values

The word 'values' is horribly over-used today, often describing the way organisations want us to believe they behave. Values language is most powerful when it influences behaviours – in other words, the way people are treated. Sometimes we recognise our values most clearly when they are challenged, such as the customer service manager who is required to make false promises and lie to customers.

Therefore, values are not just words – they are principles we live out. They are judged not by what we say but what we do. When actions and words match, we see authenticity. Knowing the difference between value statements and embedded values matters when it comes to choosing employers. Most organisations celebrate and publish their values. They say that they believe in their staff and customers and take care of the environment. How far these words translate into concrete actions varies immensely. Part of your due diligence as a job hunter is to tell the difference between organisations that engage in spin, and those that make a reasonable effort to put their stated values into practice.

We take our values to work, and judge our work by its closeness to those values. Sometimes you might be asked to do something you think is dishonest or unfair. You might witness behaviours or language you did not admire. What were your values when you began your career? How have they changed, and why? Where have your values been affirmed at work, and where have they been questioned, challenged or flattened?

## Exercise 9.2 – Challenged values

Engaging in activity which matches your personal values can provide job satisfaction. Sometimes we may feel that work is in conflict with our personal values. For example:

- You were asked to do something you didn't believe in.
- You observed behaviours or language you did not admire.
- You were asked to behave in a way that feels opposite to your personal values.

Try to remember **a day at work** where you were in a situation which did NOT match your values. Record your answers below.

| |
|---|
| What happened? |
| Why did the event challenge your values? |
| Based on this event, how would you describe your values? |

# Exercise 9.3 – Exploring your values in more depth

Use the following question sequence to identify your values. Share the results of this with someone you trust who is interested in your development.

## Step 1 – Behaviours and attitudes you find unattractive

What qualities and attitudes in others do you dislike? (Some words to start you thinking: *judgemental, intolerant, lazy, arrogant*.) List these qualities, then in the bottom box record how you wish people would behave.

| | |
|---|---|
| Behaviours and attitudes I don't admire | |
| How I wish my least favourite people would behave | |

## Step 2 – Role models

Who are the people you admire and respect most? These may be famous people, family members, friends, work colleagues. What qualities and attitudes are shown by these people? (Think of *how* they live and work, not just what they've achieved.) Write your answers down below. (Some words to start you thinking: *modest, risk-taking, self-sacrificing, entrepreneurial, caring, creative, brave, honest, challenging, encouraging, ethical, reliable, consistent*.)

| |
|---|
| What qualities and attitudes do you admire most in other people? |

## Step 3 – Organisational values

Think about organisations you know well, including ones you have worked for:

> What values do you admire most in these organisations?

## Step 4 – Your top 6 values

Identify any positive values recorded above. Highlight the six words that matter to you most and record them here:

| My top 6 values | |
|---|---|
| 1 | 4 |
| 2 | 5 |
| 3 | 6 |

You can use this list in a number of ways. You can actively look for organisations or sectors where these values will be matched. If you're offered a role, you can use background research to find out about the organisation's real values.

## 'Must do' list

Questions to help you reflect on your personality and working style:

- ✓ What brings you to life? When or where do you become energised? What has a deadening effect on you?
- ✓ What work environments suit you best? What kind of intelligence do you bring to the workplace?
- ✓ How far might your next career step require you to work on self-awareness, resilience or improved interpersonal skills?
- ✓ How well can you anticipate what a psychometric test will reveal about you?
- ✓ What preparation do you need to do to be ready to answer questions on how you operate under pressure, or your strengths and weaknesses?
- ✓ What are your values, and what kind of work would match them best?

# Identifying work that feels worth doing

'Find a job you like and you add five
days to every week.' **H. Jackson Browne**

*This chapter helps you to:*

- Understand why it's difficult to choose a career path
- Find out about kinds of work you know nothing about at present
- Identify jobs and sectors for investigation
- Use lateral thinking to help you to identify new areas of work
- Draw all your discoveries together.

## Choices, choices

Think of the billions of people who have lived on this planet throughout history, and the seven billion who live on it today. According to some calculations, about one in ten of all the people who ever lived are alive today. The reason is obvious – there are more of us, and we're living longer. This 10% slice of human history has more life choices and more work choices available to it than any previous generation. Even three generations ago, the average European worker probably had about five to ten obvious occupations to choose from. Today, there are tens of thousands of occupations available, but we're still using the same brain as earlier generations – we don't have a new mental toolkit to help us choose.

More than a few people wonder *what would be my dream job?* This question, of course, relies heavily on the idea that there might be a single, 'right' path for each of us, and some people believe that a simple career test will reveal the answer. We live in a society that wants choices about everything, so there is real pressure to find the 'perfect' job. This book will show you that having a job you love needn't be about waiting for your dream job to come along. The answer is usually about finding work that is a healthy match to who you are.

### Sectors – and choosing them more carefully

Workers today have much broader choices than any previous generation. How do we deal with these choices? First of all, we need to learn to draw maps of what is out there, which means understanding fields. One sensible way of looking at jobs is to categorise them into groups and subgroups. Imagine an office block full of filing cabinets. Every type of job in the world you can imagine, from Aardvark Handler to Zebra Painter, has its own file. To make sense of all these files, you would want to group related jobs together in one place. This is what we mean by fields of work or, as we describe them here, *sectors*. Some sectors are huge, such as health. Within that large 'job family' are several smaller sectors, including nursing. But even if you choose nursing, you will soon have to decide on a main focus, and also on the likely workplace.

### Discovering what enlivens, and what dampens

The main reason you are unhappy in your work may be due to the people you work with. It may be environmental: you don't like your place of work or the journey that takes you there. These can all alter (change of boss, relocation) without your role changing at all. You may be out of tune with the organisation – particularly if you don't share its values (see Chapter 9).

Some people are happy in their role no matter which sector they work in. Would you enjoy doing the role you do in a different sector? Someone who enjoys networking computers, for example, probably doesn't mind doing the job in a factory, hospital or office building. Others are dissatisfied with work – but don't realise that they haven't yet found a sector which feels interesting.

### Resources for investigation

How do we discover what sectors exist, and what it's really like to work in them? In the past we had to rely on careers libraries, but today a wealth of information is a mouse click away. Investigate sectors and jobs using comprehensive sites such as prospects.ac.uk/job-profiles. Research organisations thoroughly, noting the titles of jobs you see mentioned. Check out online video interviews (for example, careersbox.co.uk) where people talk about their jobs. Websites such as www.glassdoor.com can be a good starting point for learning about organisation cultures and why people leave or stay (check out a range of opinions, and make sure they're up to date and supported by your own personal investigations).

## Why sectors are powerful

Sector choice can be a powerful route to an inspired career, influencing a range of factors:

- the kind of people you work with and the things that matter to those people;

- the skills you will be using, and the skills valued by the organisation;
- the skills you will be using, and the skills valued by the organisation;
- the main purpose of the organisation;
- the main focus of your working activity;
- the values underlying the work that is performed;
- the likely speed of change in the job, and how much learning you have to do.

### Sectors and funnels

Society likes to put information and ideas into compartments, beginning at school. You didn't have classes entitled *Thinking, Speaking, Imagination* or *Wisdom* (you might have done if we still followed Renaissance ideas about education). In the Victorian age, educators reclassified what was taught into narrower boxes (and at the same time invented new subjects, including English and Physics). We choose between the arts and sciences, with very little crossover between the two.

The subjects you learn in the classroom prompt further courses of study. They also *seem* to suggest career paths. If you have academic strengths in one area, a certain number of obvious careers come to mind: 'I'm good at science, so I should be a scientist.' The problem here is only broad pathways are indicated (for example, 'finance', 'law', 'business', 'computers'). Knowing that there is a wide range of well-paid jobs out there which fit under these very general headings, we continue our studies with optimism, even if the direction is vague.

Some early indications are rather more negative. If you're good at languages, for example, you'll think about being a translator, teaching or possibly working in export/import. Beyond that you may run out of ideas. If you're a child who is good at music, art or drama, well-meaning relatives will doubtless remind you of the fact that artists in these fields often struggle to make a living. Options close down quickly, and soon you're drifting towards 'sensible' subjects and jobs, even though these routes are less exciting.

This early game of career snakes and ladders describes much of what goes on when we choose subjects at school. It's easy to make the assumption that taking the right subjects will move you into the 'right' career. This promise of 'educational funnelling' is the basis of early career thinking. We really do give young people a sense that when they narrow down their choices, for example at A-level, they are becoming more focused in career terms. Every year we turn out thousands of newly qualified people who have no idea how to make their qualifications relevant to employers (see Chapter 17). Few degree subjects outside science and technology are *directly* related to the jobs that graduates will actually perform.

Your secondary education narrowed your studies down to around 10 subjects, but there are literally thousands of sectors of knowledge and work out there, and few of them have a direct link to school subjects – there are few people practising 'pure' geography, history or mathematics in the world, and there are many top-level generalists.

We're distracted by two very lazy bits of thinking. The first is viewing the world in terms of occupational titles. When a kindly uncle pats his six-year-old niece on the head and asks 'What do you want to do when you grow up?', the question clearly requires a job title as an answer. We're expected to choose the right label very early without knowing anything much about work. Later in life, in social situations, you're asked 'What do you do?' – again, seeking a job title. We'd get very different results asking questions about what people enjoy, and what their ideal mix of tasks would look like (see the Jigsaw Job exercise in Chapter 3).

### Sectors and motivation

It's easy to choose a sector that seems 'safe'. At times of crisis you will be attracted by sectors where you can operate inside protective boundaries – your comfort zone. It's common among career changers to hear them say, 'I would really like to work in a sector which inspires me, but I will find it much easier to get a job in the sector I have been working in for the last 20 years.'

Talk to people who love the sector they have found themselves in. People in this situation are often happy to talk about their work. Generally, they are interested in more than the role they occupy. They have a broader interest in what colleagues do, and where their organisation fits into the bigger picture. They encourage others to follow the path they have taken. Once you find a sector that gives you the same 'buzz', you will approach both your job search and the work you do far more positively. The spin-offs, both for yourself and for any organisation which employs you, are important:

- You will be more enthusiastic at interviews – and employers love enthusiasm.
- You will retain what you learn and enjoy passing knowledge on to colleagues.
- Your love of your work will communicate itself to clients and increase their loyalty.
- You will find it far easier to fit into an organisation where others share your passion.
- Efficiency and productivity will come naturally to you.
- You will be forever interested in new ideas, new connections, and increasing your learning.

# Sector problems

### Problem 1: Not knowing what's out there

Choosing from unknown careers is like trying to plan a journey using a road atlas full of blank pages. Sector discovery helps to draw the missing maps.

If you can't find a sector that suits you, then you may have to find a new angle. Work is changing so rapidly that new disciplines are being created all the time. Maybe you'll dream up an entirely new sector. Before Galileo, there really wasn't a discipline you could describe as experimental physics. The word 'scientist' wasn't invented until the 1830s. Before Freud, there wasn't a sector called psychoanalysis. The world wide web was made available to the public in 1991, but took several years to become established. The internet as we know it today has transformed the way we work and creates new kinds of jobs every week, and it's still a new phenomenon. Something that has transformed society has only been around, in human terms, for a heartbeat.

'The best way to predict the future is to invent it.'   **Alan Kay**

### Problem 2: Starting with the wrong idea

A huge amount of the information we hold about sectors of work comes second-hand. We rely on out-of-date information from family, colleagues, and friends. The problem is that most of this information is filtered and interpreted by someone else, and probably out of date. It doesn't give you an overview of the job.

The second problem is that what we see is weighted. When people describe jobs to us, they attach value tags (safe/risky, dull/exciting, boring/cutting edge, fixed/changing). Sometimes this information is entirely accurate, providing you with really important clues about what work is actually like. Often this advice is out of date, subjective – or just plain wrong.

The first principle is to start with your own impulse, not with someone else's idea of what a job is like. Find out for yourself. Don't rely on the slanted, possibly jaded views of retired professionals, recruiters or friends.

And remember that *the* great question to ask someone doing any job is this: *What do you do most of the time?*

### Problem 3: Choosing too narrow a range

The problem with looking at sectors is that they are just ideas in boxes. They can provide a very helpful filter in terms of identifying jobs that would suit you. For example, you may have a very clear idea that your work needs to be in education, or at least in learning and development. However, choosing this way can also be restrictive. It's easy to choose sectors that are obvious and established, and miss new, growing or changing sectors.

Watch out for a blinkered, over-optimistic reliance on a particular sector. Let's say your interest is in forestry. You like working outdoors in the wild woods. You go through the training which adds to your depth of background knowledge about forestry and conservation. You get a job. You find yourself dealing with peripheral problems such as record-keeping, litter or car parks. You find that less and less of your knowledge and enthusiasm is being tapped, and you are increasingly learning about regulations, funding, and government initiatives: possible career crisis. You find yourself saying, 'I came into forestry because I love conservation and wildlife, but I've become a bureaucrat.' I hear the same story almost every week from people in teaching, HR, nursing, travel, university lecturing, and ministry. What I hear is this: 'I was attracted by the box called nursing, and I liked what it said on the label: caring for people, being there for patients and relatives. What am I now? A form filler.'

One characteristic about people who have made huge, brave career changes is that they became excited about what they didn't know, and started to do something about the gap in their knowledge. You only begin to know what's out there by being fascinated by what's out there. Active exploration, not endless reflection, is the key to career matching.

### Problem 4: How do I know if I'll like it?

This question gives away an assumption: *the only way to find out about a job is to take it and see if it works out.* It's worth reading that last sentence again. Taking a job to discover if you like it is one of the nation's favourite career strategies. Too many candidates experiment by taking a job because it looks acceptable (or it's the first one to come along), and hoping for the best.

No one should ever take a job thinking they know next to nothing about the sector or organisation. In fact, it's vital to find out well before the interview stage. Research of this kind makes you a more credible candidate, but also reveals whether the role is likely to be a good long-term fit. Active investigation like this requires that you do more than simply apply for roles; you seek information not hunches, and you find out for yourself what sectors, organisations, and roles are really like.

### Problem 5: Moving on from subjects to sectors to choices

A common place where my clients get stuck is that they identify subject areas that interest and inspire them, but they can't make a connection between a subject of interest (for example, history) and a sector of work. They succumb too quickly to 'either/or' thinking (see Chapter 4): sectors are *either* for work *or* pleasure. Friends might suggest you 'follow this interest in your spare time'. Most of us work such long hours that spare time interests are often put on the back burner for several years. You might also be asked, 'if you do what you love for a living, won't you get sick of it?' Again this ignores the experience of all those people who describe work as an enjoyable, central part of life.

If you can't see how you can move from subjects you love to potential sectors of work, you need to do some work on ways of making connections.

## Identifying sectors that will interest and inspire you

Begin with yourself. Look back at your House of Knowledge in Chapter 8. What subjects, topics, and themes energise you? What do you love learning or talking about? What do you want to know more about?

Draw on the three exercises in this chapter to work out sectors that interest you. Look at the sectors you write down. Are they really sectors at all ('consultancy' isn't a sector, but a way of working). Are your sectors too big? If necessary, convert sectors into sub-sectors. For example, if your sector is marketing, ask yourself what products or services you are interested in marketing. How is the sector described? What about sub-sectors – what terms are used within the industry to describe them? Vagueness quickly communicates itself to recruiters; using the correct terms shows you're committed to doing your homework.

# Exercise 10.1 – Prompts to get you thinking about sectors

## Stage 1: Remembering

1. Jobs you imagined doing in your childhood. What sectors do they suggest?
2. The most enjoyable subjects you've studied.
3. Sectors where you have had some work experience.
4. Sectors which appeal to you when they are portrayed in documentaries or articles.
5. Jobs done by friends or family which you find fascinating.
6. Advertised posts that attracted you, even if you never applied for them.

## Stage 2: Three great days at work

7. Think about a time when you had a great day at work. The sort of day where everything went well and you went home energised. Write down what you were doing, what you enjoyed and what you achieved.
8. Do the same thing for another two memorable days.

## Stage 3: Imagining

9. What jobs have you ever imagined doing?
10. If you could try someone else's job for a day, what would it be?
11. If you could do any job in the world for a week and still receive your normal salary, what jobs would you try?
12. Who are your role models or champions, and what sectors are they in?

## If I could do anything . . .

If you're discussing career choices with a friend, a common question is, 'what if you could do *anything*?' or, 'if you could do any job in the world for a month, what would it be?' Chapter 4 offers the variation: 'what would you do if all jobs paid the same?' If you take status and money out of the picture, you can simply focus on that key question: *what would I be doing most of the time?*

Career changers are often asked, 'what would you do if you won the lottery?' People who have won millions on the National Lottery seem to follow an interesting pattern. After playing with the money for a year or two, buying houses, holidays, and cars, they tend to get bored and look for something to do. Now that money is not the reason for working, what they choose to do is somehow even more authentic. This might mean investing in a business or starting a charitable foundation, or it might be taking up a simple trade. One lottery winner went back to his job as a staff trainer for McDonald's restaurants. So, if you win the lottery, what will you do two years later when you're bored?

'An idea that is not dangerous is unworthy of being called an idea at all.' **Oscar Wilde**

### Pushing sector alternatives

The ability to push for alternatives is a powerful thinking skill. The mind has a natural tendency to seek certainty and security, and sometimes finds alternatives uncomfortable. A training colleague used to have a phrase for this: 'Don't confuse me with facts, my mind is made up.'

You might feel that your thinking should follow a logical sequence: problem – analysis – solution. This logical process may seem the best way forward, but there are dangers. Career changers love tests, boxes, and checklists. Their brain is saying, 'I feed the data in *here*, and the answer pops out *here*. It's tempting to sit back and wait for a computer test to sample your interests and aspirations and name suitable job titles. These tests don't look at the full range of things that makes a career work for you, including your personality, values, and motivated skills. Additionally, tests that generate job titles have no hope of keeping up with the wide range of jobs available. Tests should only ever be used to prompt exploration, never to dictate.

At first glance, having too many alternatives might seem a recipe for indecision. Brainstorming is one of the best tools used to prompt business creativity, but this is often misused because the process is cut off halfway through. Brainstorming is a good way of generating a large number of ideas in a free-flowing, non-critical environment. The effect is rather like a shotgun blast: broad and inaccurate. What any brainstorming session needs (and this will apply to your own creative thinking applied to the career process) is a secondary tool to help you to prioritise, test ideas, group ideas together, and focus on the next step.

### Confidence

Notice that moment of hesitation before you write down the name of a sector. Look at what's going on in your head. *I'll never get into this sector. I don't have the training. I don't know enough.* In those moments remember this: US President Abraham Lincoln carried with him everywhere a newspaper clipping stating that he was a great leader. John Lennon's school report read, 'certainly on the road to failure'. We all need a little more encouragement.

### Switching sectors: the practicalities

Building on a formula popularised by Richard Nelson Bolles, here is an overview of the graduated difficulties of career change:

1. It is relatively straightforward to remain in the same sector but change occupation. For example, you may remain

in higher education but become a lecturer rather than an administrator.

2. It is relatively straightforward to remain in the same occupation, but switch sector – for example, remain an accountant – but switch from manufacturing to the hotel trade.

3. The hardest shift is to change both occupation and sector at the same time. Don't believe those negative voices that tell you this is impossible. You just need better research, and a better strategy for finding out what's really out there. Sometimes it's worth thinking about a stepping-stone approach: change one element now, and another in, say, 12 months' time, when you have gained some relevant experience.

'What work I have done I have done because it has been play. If it had been work I shouldn't have done it.' **Mark Twain**

### One-step-at-a-time career breakthrough

Many self-help books will try to persuade you that we all have a hidden, 'real' self, and if we can unlock this secret, then the answer to the question 'what should I do with my life?' will become crystal clear. The popular press reinforces the idea that deep down we all have a single dream job, and what we long for is an overnight transformation. That's why newspapers love stories of 'accountant becomes skydiver' or 'commando becomes nanny'.

In fact, such transformations are relatively rare. More frequently, people progress by gradual steps; they 'try on' careers experimentally. Many do this in their first ten years of work, when it's relatively easy to change direction and experiment. We often write off this period of our life as uncertain 'drifting'. The idea that we are more likely to make incremental than dramatic career changes was explored in depth in Herminia Ibarra's book *Working Identity* (Harvard Business Review Press, 2004).

Jim Bright takes a different approach. He has famously applied 'chaos theory' to careers work (see *The Chaos Theory of Careers* by Robert Pryor and Jim Bright (Routledge, 2011) and www.brightandassociates.com.au). Bright suggests that random events play a much bigger part in our careers than we believe; we often look back at decisions and rationalise them, but at the time they were improvised responses to a complex and unpredictable world. Jim Bright's research found that about three-quarters of people, including students, have changed direction because of an unplanned event. This work argues that we get more out of our careers where we seek out new experiences rather than trying to plan and predict (see 'Be more experimental' on p. 60).

If you want a career breakthrough, commit time to exploring sectors of interest, and keep an open mind. Chapter 11 will help deepen your thinking about options.

Making a huge leap in your career is not straightforward. This is particularly true if this involves a change of sector (for example, moving from events management to sports coaching) or a major change of lifestyle (for example, from financial director to author). It's a risky process (as people will take delight in reminding you) because it's about moving from known to unknown. It helps to begin with subjects that fascinate you.

## Exercise 10.2 – From subjects of interest to occupational sectors

| Subjects that interest me | Obvious matching sectors | Not so obvious sectors | Wild ideas | Example organisa-tions |
|---|---|---|---|---|
| Creative writing | Copywriting, journalism | Internal communications | Lobbying | |
| | | | | |
| | | | | |
| | | | | |
| | | | | |

1. List subjects that interest you. Use the House of Knowledge (Chapter 8) and Exercise 10.1 to help identify them. Add any extras that come to mind. Write them down in column 1 (an example is shown).
2. Against each subject, record at least two **obvious matching sectors** – for example, if you have put 'history' in column 1, obvious sectors for column 2 might include *museums, conservation*.
3. Now think of two or more **not so obvious sectors**, asking yourself, 'where else are people who know about this subject employed?' (e.g. *documentary making*). Do your homework (e.g. Google 'Career ideas for language learners').
4. Add any **wild ideas** that come to mind. Don't dismiss anything; be as imaginative as possible. Ask friends for suggestions.
5. As you (inevitably) come across names of example organisations, list them in the right-hand column.
6. Pick out target sectors for further investigation.

# Exercise 10.3 – Going deeper into sectors

## Step 1: Refining your list of sectors

1. Work on your list of sectors that interest you until you have 20 sectors. Write them out on cards.
2. Redefine any phrases that are too broad (e.g. 'Management' or 'Consultancy').
3. Split your top 20 cards between two column headings.

| **Primary sectors** Sectors I would like some contact with through work during the next 12 months | **Other sectors** Sectors which I found interesting, but don't need to be part of my work during the next 12 months |
| --- | --- |

## Step 2: Ranking sectors

4. Put your Primary sectors list in rank order – the most interesting sector should be Number 1. These are your top ten sectors for further investigation.

## Step 3: Sector combining

5. Take six sector cards which appeal to you. Put three in a row, and then three in a column, as below. Put a piece of paper between them and draw a 3 × 3 grid in the empty space. Try to come up with a sector or sub-sector to write in each of your nine blank squares. An example is shown below.

|  | **Card 1**<br>Physical fitness | **Card 2**<br>Language Translation | **Card 3**<br>Export/Import |
|---|---|---|---|
| **Card 4**<br>Creative writing | Writing creative self-help books promoting fitness | Translating novels | Writing export guides |
| **Card 5**<br>Health & Safety | Safety awareness in personal fitness regimes | Translation of specialised safety management texts | Exporting products and systems relating to safety management |
| **Card 6**<br>Ecotourism | Environmentally friendly cycling events | Translating commercial tourism ideas into ecotourism | Importing ecotourism practices from other cultures |

## Step 4: Putting ideas into action

6. Now begins a key step: research. Investigate the key information about these sectors (entry routes, qualifications and training you need, measures for success, prospects). Talk to people actually working in these sectors to find out what the job is really like.

7. Once you have researched your top five or six sectors, come back to this exercise. You will probably find that sector exploration leads you to redefine and adapt your working list. Don't think of your sectors list as definitive or fixed; think of it as a work in progress.

# Your 'must do' guide to exploring sectors

✓ Look back at your working life. What sectors have you found most satisfying? Why?

✓ Draw up a prioritised list of sectors that appeal to you. Set out a plan to investigate more about them.

✓ Talk to people in jobs. Find out how they got them. Use information interviews (see Chapter 15).

✓ Look for sector ideas in unexpected places which say something about you: your bookshelves, your photograph albums, articles you have clipped from newspapers.

✓ Become a future watcher. Read articles about how the world of work is changing. See how many new sectors and new job titles you can discover.

✓ Don't be put off if you can't find sectors which interest you – it just means that you need a new way of looking.

✓ When you've decided what you find exciting, tell people. Ask for their help.

✓ Don't allow 'yes, but' thinking to prevent further investigation of a sector that interests you.

✓ Investigate career ideas thoroughly – as if you were researching for somebody else.

✓ Use the **Master Sheet** (Appendix 1, p. 273) as an alternative way of identifying target sectors.

# How do I change career?

*This chapter helps you to:*

- Rethink the way you choose your career
- Understand the key ingredients of career matching
- Map out sectors you would like to actively research
- Take the first steps towards a total change of career.

## 'I think I need a complete change of career'

Let's tackle head-on this whole 'change of career' notion.
I'd argue that we have only one career – built up of multiple experiences that include work, learning, personal development, as well as the things that engage us outside work.
Incidentally, you will do better at interview if you talk in
these terms rather than apologising for 'changing career'
or 'switching paths' or any other loaded language which
implies that (a) there's only one, conventional way of having
a career, (b) any progress you've made is entirely accidental, and (c) you have no idea where you're going next.

So how do you begin if you want to add more colour, more
variety to your single, integrated career path? Here's an interesting fact about the world of careers advice. People prefer

to buy careers books with the words 'interview' or 'CV' or 'job search' in the title. However, when it comes to asking for help, most enquirers begin with a statement like, 'I would like to find out what else I could do' or 'I have a feeling I want to do something completely different' – questions about direction of travel rather than means of transport.

People ask for help partly because of the huge ranges of choices available in life. Making a career change is much tougher than making a job change. It's a journey into the unfamiliar that will require new information, new ways of thinking, a strong CV, and well-planned interview answers. Deciding to change career increases risk: small risks of rejection, and big risks that it will all go wrong. So, confidence and learning how to make progress without burning all of your boats are both critically important.

Many parts of this book will help you find a different career path. You have already looked at your constraints, examined your personality, skill set and knowledge base, and looked at the activities in life and sectors that give you a sense of fulfilment. You may already have a half-formed idea, matched by a sense of longing. That's where you begin. This chapter will take you forward so you start looking at – and acting on – completely new options.

## How do we decide on a career path?

When I have a first session with a client, I ask about past, present, and future. What has motivated this person in the past, both within work and outside it? What was the best job? The best organisation? What's going on right now that makes this client want a change? And then we move to 'what next?' Clients usually say they have no ideas about what they want to do, but they usually do. I think it was the US careers specialist Richard Knowdell who stated that everyone in the world knows exactly what they should be doing. The problem, he says, is that half haven't found the words to describe what they're looking for. The other half know exactly what they should be doing – but are too frightened to say it.

Let's backtrack slightly. How do we choose our career paths? As Chapter 10 revealed, we are funnelled into sectors of work by academic choices. However, many influences also shape our career choices:

**Influences that affect the way we choose career paths**

- **Parental expectations** – occupational groups tend to repeat themselves in families.
- **Parental aspirations** – pushing young people towards careers that match what parents believe to be the right kind of work.
- **Academic subjects** – what you choose to study may seem like the key to your future.
- **Money and status** – academic high-achievers are often pushed towards high-pay, high-status occupations such as law, finance or medicine.
- **Peer pressure** – doing something cool; avoiding things that look boring.
- **Advice from your first boss** – the opinion of your first-ever boss is often highly influential.
- **Personal values and beliefs** – the kind of work that seems worthwhile.
- **Media influence** – the jobs we see done on TV or in films or on YouTube.
- **Teachers and lecturers** – because of the effect of educational 'funnelling'.
- **High visibility** – jobs you see around you a great deal of the time.

- **Careers advisers** – particularly influential while you are also making study choices.
- **Work-related tests** – ranging from bona fide personality or interest inventories to something you found on the internet.
- **Personal inclination** – your strong (or vague) sense of what might work, what you are 'supposed' to be doing or what you feel called to in life.

We understand jobs that touch our lives. The first item above – parental influence – is more influential than you might think. In a November 2017 piece for *The New York Times*, Quoctrung Bui and Claire Cain Miller show how certain occupations stay in families: 'Some of the jobs most likely to be passed down include steelworker, legislator, baker, lawyer and doctor. Children are less likely to follow their parents' careers if they are middle managers or clerical or service workers.' The authors conclude that 'Children often pursue their parents' jobs because of the breakfast-table effect: family conversations influence them. They fuel interests or teach children what less commonly understood careers entail.'

Sometimes young people are touched by jobs in other ways. If you spend a lot of time in hospital in childhood, you may want to be a nurse or a doctor. In a TV programme about a remote Indian Ocean island that lacked even a school or post office, a young boy was asked what he wanted to do when he grew up. *Fishing*, he said, naming the one job he could see available to adult males.

### Work on screen

Even in our developed society, we are exposed to only a fraction of the jobs available. Do you know what a systems analyst does, or a risk assessor, an order picker, a voice coach? In our modern economy, new types of jobs are created every day. Most will be invisible to us, and we have to rely on hunches, insider information or assumptions to choose between them. Some jobs are more visible than others. You know what a surgeon, a barrister or a firefighter does. Or, you *think* you do, but how much of your perception is based on TV roles rather than the way people really do their jobs?

The influence of the media on career choice should not be overestimated. TV, in particular, samples the world of work in a very slanted way. Some jobs are never off the screen (medics, lawyers, teachers, police officers, CSIs, chefs), others shown rarely (when did you see TV fiction include an offshore rigger, 3D designer, personal shopper, car valeter, order picker?). Some occupations in the same sector are given very different weighting: TV loves architects but tends to ignore surveyors.

TV shows us a limited picture of work, and a distorted one at that. When you see a police officer on TV, either in fiction or in a documentary, what do you see? Normally the officer is chasing, apprehending or interviewing a member of the public. Talk to actual police officers and you discover that even those on the 'beat' spend most of their time doing one thing: responding to emails. TV prefers the more exciting moments: the airline pilot avoiding a crash, the lawyer bringing in a surprise witness, the GP diagnosing a mystery illness.

TV shapes the way we see jobs more than anything else, and this is concerning when viewers struggle to tell the difference between television and reality. The actor Johnny Briggs played the factory owner Mike Baldwin in *Coronation Street* for 30 years. Every week the soap star received applications seeking work in his fictional factory. Even more worryingly, about once a week someone applied for the job of assistant manager.

### Deciding what or who?

As the previous chapter has discussed, too many young people face the unimaginative question: 'What do you want to do when you grow up?' It's a question that seems to demand a single job title: 'Er . . . a . . . chartered accountant!'

A better conversation would focus on the mix of things you enjoy doing. It might also ask what kind of person you hope to *be*. Those with a more spiritual view of life choices often say the most important thing is who you are, not what you do. Others will say that self-examination is self-indulgent and we should all focus on the work that is actually available – 'ideal' and 'real' (see Chapter 4) are once again in conflict.

Looking at career possibilities, like some of the most important thinking we do, requires you to hold conflicting and overlapping ideas in your mind at the same time. The **Three Career Circles** diagram shows how this can be put to practical effect.

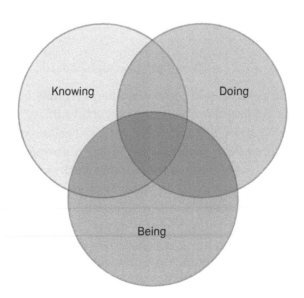

Draw a larger version of the Three Career Circles for yourself, and within each circle write in the key words that emerge from the following discussion of knowing, being, and doing.

### Knowing

Chapter 8 revealed how *what you choose to know about* provides powerful clues about meaningful work. So, if you are considering a complete change of career, think about the topics you would like to hear about at work. Review your areas of expertise, especially the underpinning knowledge you may be talking about in competency-based interviews (see Chapter 16).

Understanding the knowledge angle of work is also an insight into your motivation, both now and in the future, because it treats each job as a learning curve. Most roles are interesting in their first few weeks or months, but whether a job is intrinsically interesting in the long run is often about how much you will continue to learn and grow.

### Doing

'We are what we repeatedly do.'  **Aristotle**

Aristotle was writing about developing virtuous habits, but his words remind us of another powerful notion: *what we choose to do most of the time matters*. The activities that take up most of our waking hours have a strong influence on our effectiveness, the outcomes our work generates, and the way people see us. Remember that word 'occupation'? A job is what 'occupies' our time and attention.

Skills are powerful reinforcers of self-esteem and are the best way of making our values tangible in the world by getting things done. Skills need to be refreshed and updated, but more than anything else they need to be used. Using only part of your skill set, or using skills you really don't value very much, can lead to long-term demotivation and cynicism.

Refer to Chapter 7 to refresh your understanding of your skills and competences.

### Being

*How* you exercise skills is very highly dependent on your approach to life. To perform a task well, accurately, with care, taking into account the needs of other people, to be able to meet deadlines, to be cheerful or resourceful under pressure, these are all aspects of personality and values (see Chapter 9).

'Being' matters to a lot of people when they are choosing a career path. We're born with a range of personality traits, but we acquire attitudes, values, and ethics as we progress through life. What seems like dull work to one person can be satisfying and meaningful to someone else. Some things are demonstrated through the things we choose to learn about, others are deeper still. Think about the causes or charities you support (whether with time, money or sympathy). What issues energise you? What makes you angry?

## Career change: starting from the inside out

### What's calling you?

'Job: what you do to support your vocation.' **Anonymous**

Do you sense that you might be looking for a *vocation* rather than just than a job? The word comes from the Latin *vocare*, 'to call'. It's used most frequently in terms of a life of faith, but even in popular usage a 'vocation' feels different from an occupation. Sometimes it's used to describe a job, either professional or voluntary, that makes an important contribution to society. It also describes an occupation for which a person is specifically gifted. Not only have we redefined what we mean by 'career' in the past 50 years, we have redefined what we mean by 'vocation', too. Some feel a 'calling' towards working with animals, being a chef, creating fine art photographs, making handmade furniture, or serving in the armed forces.

When we feel 'called' to the work we do, this provides a sense of commitment stronger than ordinary levels of motivation, and a sense of 'rightness' in our choice. It's not just a strong career impulse, not just this year's big idea. To choose a vocation often implies turning your back on conventional career satisfiers such as money and status, and it is a pathway that may take years to explore and resolve. Many vocations mean a commitment of decades rather than weeks or months.

One interesting assumption is that to follow a calling means low work satisfaction: the work is about duty, not about personal choice. This is probably something worth questioning. A vocation may provide someone with a strong sense of purpose. It will probably involve some self-sacrifice. However, a vocation can also be something that is fulfilling and a good experience. 'Good experience' isn't the same as 'fun', but shouldn't be a million miles from it. Those living out vocations will admit that they are not 100% committed to their calling all of the time. The difference is they keep to the path, trying to be authentic to that original calling, and to live out long-term life choices even when things are difficult.

Peter Sinclair, originator of the 'After Sunday' movement (www.aftersunday.org.uk), is fond of reminding people that one of the clear signs of vocation is that you should look happy, at least some of the time. There are an awful lot of glum-looking people in teaching, nursing, the clergy, and charity jobs. Living a vocation may fill a useful social purpose, but if it makes you miserable, the role you're occupying is probably a poor match.

Feeling called to a particular role can provide a strong sense of 'right fit' – you've found the place which is authentically *you*. Former Archbishop of Canterbury Rowan Williams wrote: 'vocation is . . . what's left when all the games have stopped' (*A Ray of Darkness: Sermons and Reflections*, Cowley Publications, p. 152). Your calling may draw you towards the best version of yourself.

If you're uncertain whether you feel called towards a particular kind of work, there's another important consideration. A decision to follow this kind of path often arises from faith, strongly held personal values, or a sense of service. Perhaps the biggest feature of a calling is this: *it's not just about you.*

So, three tests that might help if you're wondering if you're considering a vocation rather than a job. In a vocation:

1. Your gifts are recognised by others as well as by you.
2. You commit to a long game, which may include fallow years.
3. You offer something which helps, feeds, or inspires other people. A vocation is a life lived for others.

## Career change: starting from the outside in

Are you sure you don't know what you want to do? Begin, as suggested above, with the Chapter 4 question, *what work would you do if all jobs paid the same?* Then try on the question *which jobs would you like to try out just for a week?*

Look again at the sector choices prompted by various exercises in this book, and your Work Themes (see Exercise 5.2 on p. 69). Put time aside to explore sectors that attract your curiosity. Sometimes it's easier to start with sectors that have intersected with your career to date, or sectors you're aware of through hobbies, family or friends.

Try not to allow 'yes, but' thinking to get in the way. You don't have to make a decision at this stage – all you are doing is generating ideas. Here are some other tried and tested prompts to get you to generate job ideas:

- Think of people you know who are doing interesting jobs. What's interesting about them?
- What jobs have you applied for in the past but didn't get?
- What jobs have you seen advertised that caught your attention for 30 seconds, even if you did nothing about them?

Return to your House of Knowledge in Chapter 8. The clues are all there in the topics that have called you, year after year. Stored away somewhere, in your loft or under the stairs, there's a box with the evidence: those projects that keep coming out every two or three years. Look, too, at the things you have chosen to study over the years. Chapter 10 shows you how to move from subjects that interest you to sectors of work.

Don't get hung up on another job myth: that if you try to turn a hobby into a living, you will fall out of love with it. Plenty of people are busy being paid to do things which they would happily do for nothing in their own time. Starting with subjects means starting with enthusiasm and energy. The things that fill us with happiness, no matter how trivial, are clues about activities which feed you. Sometimes it's even more important to find the things that will feed the tired soul – the kind of mid-life realignment that often matters a great deal.

'The brain is a wonderful organ. It starts working the moment you get up in the morning and does not stop until you get to work.' **Robert Frost**

## Career change: just do it

As this chapter has rehearsed, the key question is not how you are going to find a new career, but how you are going to decide on one. Thinking things through matters. Reimagining the possibilities of your career makes all the difference.

The next big question is *what are you going to do about it?* The second half of this book provides several prompts to activity, but let's nail down one plain fact. If you want to put off career change forever (or at least until it's too late), then keep on reflecting, analysing, and mulling over. Keep on thinking that you have to make the perfect decision before you act. That will happily prevent change.

If you don't want to spend your last inactive years saying 'I wish', do something – soon. Research clearly shows that you're more likely to reach goals if you have a short-term, step-by-step plan, and if you do something about step 1.

Finding out, and following your enthusiasm, costs very little. You don't need to have a perfect target job to start the process of discovery, just a sense of curiosity. And here's a big clue: your breakthrough probably has a 5% likelihood of happening as a result of reading or thinking, and a 95% likelihood of occurring as a result of a person. Someone you already know, possibly. Or, even more likely, someone you meet in the next two or three months as a result of your active enquiries. So what's the first step? A conversation. Start with people you know, even if they seem very disconnected from the world you want to enter. Find opportunities to talk to people who love what they do for a living. Experiment with REVEAL interviews (see Chapter 15).

### Pass it on

With luck and a little application you'll move towards a job you love doing. If you find what you're looking for, share your insights with other people who are at a different stage of the journey. A key part of career fulfilment is helping other people move forward.

First, you discover *your* talents – the solo instrument you play. As you continue to explore and learn, you begin to hear the other instruments people are playing around you. With time, you understand your role in the orchestra. One thing remains: to help others hear the music.

## Exercise 11.1 – The Field Generator

The **Field Generator** helps generate ideas for work sectors. You begin with things that interest you, and then follow a thought process to help you to generate ideas for new fields for you to wander into and explore.

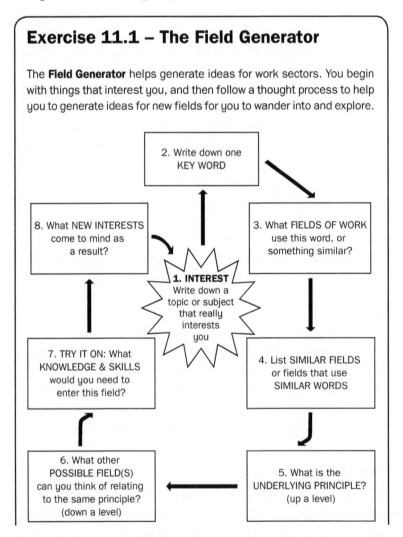

If you are short of sector ideas, go back to the House of Knowledge in Chapter 8. Use a highlighter pen to mark your preferred interests. Now use this information in the Field Generator.

| **How to use the Field Generator** | |
| --- | --- |
| **Step 1** | Make copies of the Field Generator diagram, and try this exercise out using as many interests as you can. This exercise works best with someone else working with you, prompting and asking questions. |
| | Look back at your completed House of Knowledge. Pick five or six of your strongest interests. |
| | Write one of your interests in **Box 1**, for example, boats, sailing, the sea. |
| **Step 2** | In **Box 2**, write down a key word from your area of interest, for example, sailing. |
| **Step 3** | Look at your key word and in **Box 3** write down three sectors of work where this word appears, for example, sailing instruction, sailing boat design or repair, sailing holidays. |
| **Step 4** | Now that you have expanded your sector a little, think of sectors that use similar words, and write them in **Box 4**, for example, shipbuilding, naval architecture, merchant navy, navigation. Make a note in the margin of any new fields that you hadn't thought of before that may be connected in some way with your interest, for example, outward-bound training, water safety. |
| **Step 5** | This is where you have a chance to use a technique which, in idea-building terms, is called 'going up a level'. |
| | Look at your fields in **Box 4**. Is there any overriding category that describes them? If you were to find these ideas together in one drawer, what label would you put on the front of the drawer? (For example, nursing and osteopathy can be placed within the general category of 'medicine' or 'physiology'.) This may take a while to work out, or you may think of several |

alternatives. The answer will be unique to you. In this case, you might come up with weather, racing, healthy competition, low technology, getting away from it all, being captain of my own boat . . .

What is the underlying 'big idea'? Write down your final answer in **Box 5**, for example, healthy competition might be your preferred underlying principle here.

| | |
|---|---|
| **Step 6** | In **Box 5**, we moved up a level to the underlying principle. In **Box 6**, we come down a level at a different point.<br><br>In this case, you might come up with something totally unconnected to sailing arising from 'healthy competition', for example, sports coaching, teaching kids about diet and exercise, teaching fund-raising skills to charity staff, or selling ethical financial products. Write down any ideas that appeal to you, making sure you don't try to exclude them at this stage by misguided thinking about what is 'practical'. You may discover sectors or new interests here that could one day become part of your House of Knowledge. |
| **Step 7** | Underline one of the fields or ideas generated in **Box 6**, and write it in **Box 7**. It's probably best to begin with one that has surprised you most; for example, in this case you might have come up with teaching fund-raising skills to charity staff.<br><br>Write down what you feel to be the key skills and knowledge that you would need to work in this sector. Begin by putting down what you already know, and add more by putting yourself mentally into the shoes of someone working in this area. The only way to build up an accurate picture is to find out. Ask someone already working in this sector, or do some desk research.<br><br>If this step was productive and interesting, go back to Box 6 and do the same again with any other interesting sectors. |

| **Step 8** | **Box 8** allows you to record any new areas of interest that the exercise might have brought up, for example, coaching. Take a new copy of the Field Generator and put this new interest in **Box 1**, and begin again. |
| --- | --- |

A completed **Field Generator** is shown below.

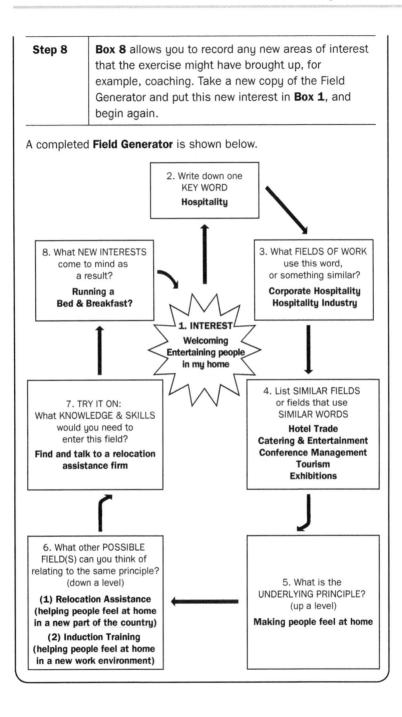

2. Write down one
KEY WORD

**Hospitality**

8. What NEW INTERESTS
come to mind as
a result?

**Running a
Bed & Breakfast?**

3. What FIELDS OF WORK
use this word,
or something similar?

**Corporate Hospitality
Hospitality Industry**

**1. INTEREST**

**Welcoming
Entertaining people
in my home**

7. TRY IT ON:
What KNOWLEDGE & SKILLS
would you need to
enter this field?

**Find and talk to a relocation
assistance firm**

4. List SIMILAR FIELDS
or fields that use
SIMILAR WORDS

**Hotel Trade
Catering & Entertainment
Conference Management
Tourism
Exhibitions**

6. What other POSSIBLE
FIELD(S) can you think of
relating to the same principle?
(down a level)

**(1) Relocation Assistance
(helping people feel at home
in a new part of the country)**

**(2) Induction Training
(helping people feel at home
in a new work environment)**

5. What is the
UNDERLYING PRINCIPLE?
(up a level)

**Making people feel at home**

## 'Must do' list

| | |
|---|---|
| **Knowing** | 1. Review what you enjoy knowing about (try the **House of Knowledge** on p. 101).<br>2. Review your preferred **work themes** (p. 69).<br>3. Use the **Field Generator** (p. 150) to translate ideas into potential sectors for investigation. |
| **Doing** | 4. Review your **skills** and achievements using Chapter 7.<br>5. Consider using the **JLA Skill Cards** to identify your motivated skills (see p. 99). |
| **Being** | 6. Look at the preferences expressed in your **Jigsaw Job** (p. 40).<br>7. List your top three **career hot buttons** (p. 87).<br>8. Review your **personality** and complete the **values** exercises in Chapter 9. |
| **Master Sheet** | 9. Transfer the results of key exercises in this book to the **Master Sheet** (Appendix 1, p. 273). |
| **Next steps** | Now *stop* reflecting and move into action steps:<br>10. Show your results to friends and colleagues. Ask for ideas.<br>11. Tell people what you think you might be looking for – use the two-breath message on p. 218.<br>12. Look for conversations to help you find out more about interesting roles, sectors, and organisations. |

**12**

# Exploring different ways of working

'If you can fall in love with what you are going to do for a living, you've got it made.' **George Burns**

*This chapter looks at:*

- Rebalancing and refreshing your career
- New choices in working arrangements
- Exploring portfolio careers
- Temporary, interim, and flexible working arrangements.

## Changing the way you think of your career

Two generations ago we enjoyed an unusually high degree of job security in return for company loyalty. Workers of the twenty-first century face a very different world. Jobs are created and lost at great speed as organisations restructure themselves frequently. A career no longer seems a simple path; it will probably be built of several strands and multiple experiences.

Management writer Charles Handy predicted the end of the 'employee society' – a decline in conventional, permanent, full-time roles, and an increase in flexible working (interim, contract, flexi-hours) and self-employment. Work no longer makes sense in traditional terms. Workers today are, for example, likely to find themselves in occupations that are not closely related to their prior qualifications and training. Even though everyone knows that jobs are no longer for life, it still comes as a surprise to have to reinvent yourself. Each year more individuals discover they have to draw their own maps.

### Career refreshment

This is a book that acknowledges the importance of finding the right kind of work. However, the job you love now may not be a job you want to do forever. Our motivations for work and our sense of the rewards we get out of it change as we grow older. Careers need to be refreshed from time to time. We are becoming increasingly attuned to the idea that we will probably change career paths several times during a working lifetime. In other words, your long-term focus may not just be on getting a job you love, but on getting a series of jobs you love, and perhaps doing some of those jobs at the same time.

## Working options

Organisations and workers are both learning to think differently about how projects are completed and work is delivered. We're all learning to think less about jobs and more about solving an organisation's problems. Increasingly, the emphasis is on the task or project, which might be delivered entirely through external or internal staff resources, or a mix of the two. As this chapter will explain, the market is increasingly less focused on job-shaped objects. Don't overestimate the impact of this: most workers in the UK are still in conventional salaried employment. According to the ONS, in January 2018 there were just over 27 million employees in the UK, and 4.78 million self-employed workers (a significant increase from the 2001 total of 3.3 million).

Whatever the totals, many workers, particularly at a professional level, have learned to think and talk about their careers not as a series of jobs, but as a series of projects, rather than as long-term relationships. Hence the rise of terms like 'giganomics': when work feels more like a 'gig' or a one-off task, your focus is on multiple clients rather than a single employer. In addition, we have seen a growth in unpaid internships, interim positions, fixed-term roles, and zero-hour contracts.

### Temporary and contract working

A significant slice of work is available on a **temporary** basis, largely through recruitment agencies. Although there are a few sectors which do not use temporary staff, most of the work available is in relatively conventional areas. So, for example, many office and reception roles are filled on a temp basis, as are a number of factory, warehouse, and processing jobs. There are defined contract markets in health, education, and transport. In other areas it's more common for work to be provided on **contract,** sometimes for several months, particularly in fields such as IT. Temp work can be a good door opener by giving you knowledge of new sectors or what it's like to work in a large organisation. You may not get access to training and career development opportunities.

If you are going to take temporary or contract work, think about what it will add to your CV. You will subsequently be asked about your choices, and to make sure that you don't get stuck in temp roles for a long period, it's important to look at the learning value of each appointment. Remember also that undertaking work on a short-term basis is often an extended audition: because your performance is a known quantity, there's a pretty good chance that you will be offered a permanent role.

However, be aware that agencies match candidates and roles very rapidly, and it's easy to be pigeon-holed in the wrong way, for example, being offered a series of repetitive temp roles that don't stretch you. Agencies often assume you want to do what you have done before. Ask for different kinds of work assignments and negotiate learning opportunities.

Those recently qualified, and some career changers, find that paid or unpaid internships offer useful short-term opportunities. See Chapter 17 for more advice.

### Interim roles

Interim work is essentially a form of short-term contract for more experienced staff. The work is provided through a wide range of interim agencies who regularly seek professionals with specialist expertise or extensive management or functional experience. The daily rate depends very much on the seniority of the last permanent job you held.

Interims can cover a short-term problem or can be retained for more than a year. Unlike a consultant, your role is not just to make recommendations, but also to implement them. There is now a wide range of interim management consultancies in the UK, and if you are thinking of working in this field, investigate what they have to offer. However, the best course of action is to talk to someone who is currently undertaking an interim assignment. Remember, too, that your most likely source of interim work is with an employer you already know.

An interim assignment is often a good way of gaining sector expertise that will allow you to move into a senior role in a new sector. These types of assignment offer a great deal of flexibility for those who want to work for part of the year and take extended breaks. The negatives are that you may have to work some distance away from home, and it's easy to become known as a 'career' interim and lose credibility as a permanent candidate.

### Flexible working

Even in a recession, employers have become far more positive about flexible working, including some degree of home working, largely because of advances in technology. You may want flexible working hours because of family responsibilities, commuting stress, or to free up time for other activities. Part-time working can assist with life–work balance, but you will probably put in more hours than you are paid for. In addition, you may be underexposed in the company and so not have a high profile with decision-makers, and therefore miss opportunities for promotion and career development offered to full-time colleagues.

Remember that a great many part-time jobs are negotiated rather than advertised, and these roles are often filled by word of mouth. Alternatively, a job that is first conceived as a full-time position may sometimes be renegotiated into a part-time role once you have proven your value.

Job shares can sometimes be the answer. However, it's nearly impossible to persuade an employer to agree to a job share unless you and your colleague are already working for the organisation. Employers are wary of set-up costs and the complexity of managing job sharers. Like part-time staff, job sharers sometimes find they are overlooked in career development terms. If your job-share partner leaves, you may find it difficult to find someone else to fill the role.

### Mixed mode: employed and self-employed

Some workers mix salaried and self-employed work. A few have more than one employer. You may gain an income from freelance or session work. Investigate alternative careers by trying out something different. This might be at the week-end, or during the evening – what some call the **5 to 9 week** rather than the 9 to 5 week (thanks to fellow career coach James Parsons for alerting me to this neat phrase). Others start businesses on a part-time basis, phasing one kind of work in and another out as the business grows.

### Negotiating something that isn't a conventional full-time job

When candidates are talking to organisations, they often learn it's best not to talk about **job-shaped objects.** In other words, focus on the problem to be solved rather than the way the job is conceived.

When talking to an organisation, don't put your needs first. If you start by saying 'I am only interested in a job that is part-time/interim/short-term . . .', you are putting the focus on the time you won't be delivering. Often this is enough to exclude you. Your main motivation to get hired appears to be finding a job that fits your lifestyle, not focusing on the needs of the organisation. Begin by finding out what an employer needs and make your usefulness clear. If the employer is interested, you *may* have the opportunity to negotiate different working arrangements to those stated. Some employers would rather have someone on a flexible basis than miss out on the right skills; others are attracted by the ability to reduce overhead costs. If they want you, things become negotiable, including working conditions.

## A portfolio career

What is a 'portfolio' career? The term is used to describe a deliberate choice to mix and match different work modes to find an effective balance. In the past, well-funded company pension schemes allowed executives to retire early and build a portfolio to keep them active during their final decade or so of working. Today's portfolio worker may have several drivers, including income, variety, and the difficulties and restrictions of salaried roles. Some hold down three or four appointments simultaneously, such as an IT consultant who also works as a board member of a health trust, a non-executive director of a publishing company, and a charity trustee. Some use high-paid working days to subsidise other work, for example, a marketing specialist who works for two days a week at corporate rates, the rest as a lecturer. Examples vary enormously: a self-employed joiner who buys and sells antiques as a side-line, a part-time HR specialist who works as a freelance book editor, an in-house lawyer who runs her own business as an equal opportunities trainer. Some of these people might not automatically recognise themselves as 'portfolio workers', but they are living examples of a new, pragmatic and highly inventive method of working.

In recent years, portfolio working has attracted a great deal of attention. As indicated above, self-employment and part-time working remain important features in the UK and many other economies. Much of the increase in self-employment has been among those aged 50 and above.

In the 1990s, only about 10% of executive career changers I was working with were interested in portfolio working. Today, it's more like 50% of men and women in this client group over the age of 50. Younger people, too, are adopting the approach – sometimes out of necessity – as Barrie Hopson and Katie Ledger make clear in their very practical book *And What Do You Do? 10 Steps to Creating a Portfolio Career* (A & C Black, 2009).

What kind of people benefit from this new working method? People who enjoy variety and change. People who have become dispirited by the constraints of a conventional career, lack of variety or growth. One of the great advantages of portfolio work is that you're not at the whim of a single organisation. You probably won't be made redundant, and if one income stream stops, you have others already in place. The exciting thing about portfolio work is its unpredictability: you never know what kind of project or enquiry is coming in next, and you may be doing an entirely different mix of work in 12 months' time.

**Exploring new ways of working**

1.  Look seriously at how many things on your wish list you could achieve in a **conventional job** (for example, running your own profit centre within a larger organisation).
2.  **Look before you leap.** Find people who have made a similar move. If it's a competitive sector, find people to talk to in other parts of the country.
3.  Work out what **draws you** towards self-employment and what **pushes you away** (see Exercise 12.1 below).
4.  Think hard about how you are going to **promote yourself.** How will people find you?
5.  Plan ahead for **isolation** – recruit friends and mentors to support you, and network with people doing the same kind of work to swap stories and exchange ideas.
6.  Focus on your **offering** – what product or service will you offer? How will it be different (cheaper, better, quicker, smarter) than others available?
7.  **Don't get hung up on the frills.** It's great fun equipping your office, printing your own business cards, and setting up your own website, but none of this matters as much as your first piece of work. Look hard at where your first business transactions are going to come from.

8.  Pin down your **first three clients.** If you have three customers lined up who will pay for your services, no questions asked, you probably have a business. Don't get hooked on the business idea: look for an income stream.

### Beginning a portfolio career

The market doesn't offer you the chance of becoming a portfolio worker. It's not a role you can apply for. You might, however, begin a portfolio career as a result of a single request: if an organisation wants some of your time on a day-rate basis, you can start to think about how you are going to fill the rest of your week. This might not just be all about work – personal development and family time might be important ingredients too.

Dig deep in terms of possible elements in the mix. If you are already used to changing jobs rapidly and coping with varied income levels, the transition may be relatively painless. Think now, at the start of your exploration, about how you will fill your dance card so that you are busy and earning enough. If you plan it right, the work will find you, but that means you have to invest a great deal of time and energy initially into making a great range of contacts (see Chapter 15 on networking as part of organised discovery). Learn how to talk about what you do: explaining your distinctive work mix, and actively seeking out people who can help you to find customers and other kinds of contact.

Talk to people who have made the journey before you. Talk to people who have successfully reinvented the work they do. The reality may not be as glamorous as you think. If you are head over heels in love with an idea, speak to at least one person who is thinking of getting out of that line of business. Find out why, then match that with a balancing conversation with someone who loves their new career. If you want to move back into permanent work later in your career, you will need to prepare a good interview answer about this segment of your work history.

## Exercise 12.1 – Should I work for myself?

You might be considering self-employment, or perhaps finding a way to mix consultancy, contracting, volunteering, and other work in a portfolio career. How will you know if this career path is right for you?

The following questionnaire is designed to help you look at the pros and cons of such a move, looking at a mix of personal and practical considerations. Give each item a score between 0 'Disagree or Not Relevant' and 3 'Strongly Agree'.

| Score how strongly you respond to each of the following statements. | Disagree or Not Relevant 0 point | Mildly agree 1 point | Agree 2 points | Strongly Agree 3 points |
|---|---|---|---|---|
| 1. I'd worry that I'd only be as good as the last project I looked after | | | | |
| 2. I enjoy being considered an expert | | | | |
| 3. I need positive feedback and encouragement from colleagues and worry that I wouldn't receive that | | | | |
| 4. I feel it will improve my life–work balance | | | | |
| 5. I will always be worried about lack of long-term security | | | | |

| | | | | |
|---|---|---|---|---|
| 6. I prefer to be master of my own fate rather than subject to the whims of an organisation | | | | |
| 7. I worry about having to constantly seek new business | | | | |
| 8. I will enjoy working for a variety of customers/client organisations rather than one employer | | | | |
| 9. I will miss the support structures of a large organisation | | | | |
| 10. I will value being in control of quality in every aspect of my business | | | | |
| 11. I don't want to deal with my own accounts and taxation | | | | |
| 12. I want to get away from bureaucracy and meetings | | | | |
| 13. I am concerned that working on my own might feel lonely | | | | |
| 14. I will enjoy working more on my own and being able to think and plan more effectively | | | | |

| | | | | |
|---|---|---|---|---|
| 15. I need positive feedback and encouragement from colleagues and worry that I wouldn't receive that | | | | |
| 16. I feel it will give me an opportunity to increase my earnings | | | | |
| 17. I'm concerned about times when the money doesn't come in | | | | |
| 18. I will enjoy being able to translate hard work directly into earnings | | | | |

| | |
|---|---|
| Add up your scores for all the **even number** questions (shaded text). These answers give clues about the factors which **draw you towards** self-employment and possibly a portfolio career. | (T) Total **Towards** Score: |
| Add up your scores for all the **odd number** questions. These answers give clues about the factors which may **push you away from** self-employment and a portfolio career. | (A) Total **Away From** Score: |
| Subtract your **(A) Away From** score from your **(T) Towards** score. | Difference **T – A** Score: |

### Interpreting your results

An overall score difference of +6 or above generally indicates a strong inclination towards working outside conventional employment. Even so, look carefully at the negative factors. What might get in the way of success? What can you work on?

Where you have a score close to zero, or even a negative score, and you are still interested in self-employment, you will probably want to review both positives and negatives in some detail. What does in fact draw you to self-employment? Are there factors not listed above?

Whatever your score, look carefully at those negative factors (odd number questions) where you have scored 2 or 3. What could you do to decrease the strength of these factors?

Now that you have a sense of the balance between the things that attract you to self-employment and the things that get in the way, look at the individual items in both parts of the questionnaire that you scored most highly.

What can you do to **increase** the strength of the things that **motivate** you towards self-employment or consultancy? What can you do to **decrease** the strength of the things that **dissuade** you from consultancy or portfolio working?

# 'Must do' list: exploring a portfolio career

✓ Describe your ideal portfolio career. Write down what you would be doing during a typical month.
✓ Focus on the steps you would need to take to make it happen.
✓ Research your escape route: talk to people who have left your profession recently.
✓ Be better informed about key changes in the way people work, and the impact of new technology and new working methods.
✓ Think again about what you recognise as a career and a 'proper' job.
✓ Investigate the different routes others have taken towards portfolio careers.
✓ Talk to people who have made the journey before you. Talk to people who have successfully reinvented the work they do. Use REVEAL interviews (see Chapter 15).
✓ Ignore market myths. Find out for yourself.
✓ Weigh up the real pros and cons of change. How can you minimise the risk and maximise your return?
✓ Watch out for the crippling power of 'yes, but' thinking.
✓ Distinguish dream from reality. If a new career or enterprise interests you, find out what you will be doing most of the time.

# 13

## Smarter job searching

'An idea is nothing more nor less than a new combination of old evidence.' **James Webb Young**

*This chapter helps you to:*

- Avoid rookie job search mistakes
- Understand what will extend, or shorten, your job search
- Discover the hidden job market
- Develop a multi-channel job search strategy
- Build productive relationships with recruitment consultants.

## Your confidence window

When you're looking for a new role, time matters. Some jobs don't come along very often. Research, making connections online, and persuading people to meet you – these activities all take time.

Time matters for another reason – fading confidence. Many people go to the market too quickly, pitching themselves at jobs they don't understand with an unconvincing CV. They feel initially optimistic, but start to hit brick walls – sometimes rejection messages, often just silence. They start tinkering with their CVs (without really knowing what to change) and begin to feel less confident.

## Confidence window

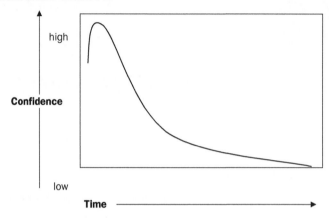

People commonly experience a confidence window like the one shown above. Initially, everything seems highly achievable. As you complete your CV and start applying for jobs, your confidence may even increase. This optimism can be rapidly dampened. You may apply online for a role and hear nothing in reply. You meet a recruitment agency who says they can't place you. Friends and family tell you to 'take what you can get' (remember those limiting voices in Chapter 2?). You start to feel that you don't have what employers want. You network a little, but do it badly, and decide it's a waste of time. Your interview performance starts to go off the boil. You're tempted to apply for any role you see.

There is good news. Confidence can be reinforced at every stage, and it's not too late to begin right now. If your job hunting isn't working, press 'pause'. Get some help to work out what you can do better. If you've only just started looking for a job, reflect on how you normally respond to rejection. You could copy the way writers proudly collect rejection slips, turning the process into a game. Or you could plan to spend time with supportive friends when you experience 'no'.

Confidence can and must be protected. That's one of the main reasons for building a support team (see Chapter 4).

It's also a healthy reminder that your best energy comes in the first few weeks of the process, which may be the time you make most impact. So why waste that time making rookie mistakes?

## Why do smart people make rookie mistakes?

No matter what new electronic tools are available, we keep making the same mistakes when job searching. Even in a tight market, candidates submit indifferent CVs. Others talk themselves out of the job in the first minutes of an interview, or fail to undertake the most basic preparation. As outlined in Chapter 1, looking for a job looks not just tedious but deceptively simple. Although there's clear evidence of what works – and what doesn't – even experienced candidates make it up as they go along. Look at the mistakes people make in the first month of job searching. They pitch themselves at large, well-known organisations. They email out vague, untested CVs to all their contacts.

At workshops, I will often list the behaviours and strategies which *extend* job searching.

### Activities likely to make your job hunt LONGER

How many of the following dead-end strategies are you currently adopting?

- Relying solely on the internet to find jobs.
- Applying for jobs without knowing why they interest you.
- Pursuing only advertised positions (when you are easily in competition with hundreds).
- Applying for jobs you don't really want 'just for the experience' (and yet feeling flattened by rejection).
- Chasing jobs in declining sectors (rather than seeking out the sectors and organisations that are experiencing growth).

- 'Lowering your sights' when things go wrong.
- Using up all your best contacts in the first three weeks and then complaining because you don't know anybody.
- Submitting a CV full of clichés, empty claims – and lacking solid evidence of achievement.
- Going to interviews with an under-rehearsed, vague performance.
- Networking without knowing why you're doing it or what you want to say.
- Jumping into a job search without undertaking proper, human-based, research.
- Spending too much time looking at screens, and not enough time with people – approaching potential contacts by email rather than by phone.
- Applying for random jobs with random messages.
- Aiming high and then low (see below).

### Activities likely to make your job hunt SHORTER

How many of the following positive strategies are you adopting?

- Shaping and road testing your CV thoroughly before you send it to important contacts.
- Carefully rehearsing what you want to say about yourself, especially before getting in front of important people.
- Using social media to research people and organisations, make connections, and build new relationships.
- Developing online exchanges into telephone conversations or face-to-face meetings.
- Networking of any kind – even just talking to friends and neighbours about job ideas can make a difference.
- Conducting information interviews (see Chapter 15) so you get under the skin of target sectors and really understand what they are looking for.

- Using your best contacts at the right time – approaching senior people who are great door openers only when you're clear how they can help, and you can give them two or three reasons why they should recommend you.
- Telling everyone you know what you're looking for, keeping it focused and simple (see 'two breath message' on p. 218).

### The high/low game

Career changers of all generations, but especially market entrants, operate in high/low mode. For example, graduates apply to high-profile employers, forgetting that these organisations are swamped with applications. Having failed to get onto the shortlist for one or two 'five-star' jobs, they aim lower – much lower. They apply for low-profile, less interesting roles, which feel easier to get. They apply for jobs which could be done by someone with far less experience or qualifications. They begin to talk themselves into taking whatever comes along.

In today's market this can mean taking a role that adds little to your CV and gives you problems in years to come. You're unlikely to get shortlisted for attractive roles in well-known organisations – especially if you apply cold without knowing what buttons to press. But if you can't persuade doors to open for five-star opportunities, dig deeper to find out how you can get closer to four-star or three-star roles.

### Smarter searching

Don't go to the market too soon, with indifferent material. The state of preparation recruitment consultants call 'market readiness' means you're ready to make the most of any opportunities that arise. More than anything, avoid random and desperate applications for jobs that mean nothing to you. Remember the idea of deal-making in Chapter 4 – look for a healthy compromise between availability and fit.

Don't spend the first three months of searching recovering from basic mistakes. Avoid situations where negative results are guaranteed – for example, going to agencies when you're unclear about the role you're seeking. Tap into your early energy. Start talking to people, certainly, but begin by talking to friends and colleagues who are supportive and easy to approach. Practise talking about yourself – particularly your areas of uncertainty – before others turn the spotlight on you. This will make you more focused and less nervous in the first round of interviews.

For a structured, step-by-step approach to job seeking, see my book *Just the Job!*

## Six steps to a smarter job search

1. **Work out your story.** Learn how to communicate why you are on the market at the moment, but also your career story as a whole – if you don't make sense of your skills and experience, an employer won't.
2. **Set out your stall.** Make a list of projects completed, tasks attained, achievements you're proud of, skills and supporting evidence, know-how, supporting qualifications and training. Catalogue your best material and use the highlights as the main features whenever you summarise what you do.
3. **Benchmark yourself against jobs.** Use the internet to research the names of jobs you hope to chase, and the skills and qualities they're looking for. Start to make your own evidence match, in terms of skill level and the language you use to describe what you're good at.
4. **Deal with problem material.** Make sure your CV covers gaps in your history, your experience, your qualifications – explain why you should still be considered.

**5. Market test.** Find people with hiring experience to give your CV a cold read, and practise your interview performance thoroughly before you get into a selection process.
**6. Broadcast on all channels.** Use a multi-strategy job search (see below) to discover, reach out, and get yourself in front of decision-makers.

## Job market myths

Let's debunk some classic myths. First, **it's easiest to do everything online**. As Chapter 14 explains, the internet is not the magic tool it seems. The web is a great tool for researching organisations and opening doors, but just applying online is a slow and frustrating process. So, think again about the idea that you should **look mainly for advertised jobs**. Chapter 1 outlined the way jobs have slipped off the radar screen into the hidden job market. Advertised positions attract hundreds of applications, making it very hard to stick out from the crowd. In addition, someone may be the preferred candidate even before the job is advertised.

**You'll be told it's better to look for a job when you have one already.** Employers are highly influenced by recent experience and the ability to bring skills online quickly, so your most recent work history helps. However, organisations restructure all the time and many candidates are 'between jobs'. If you've been out of a role for a while, provide evidence of how you've kept your skills up to date.

**Some believe that qualifications are vital.** In fact, employers often have only a vague sense how qualifications translate into employable skills. Apply what you can do to the needs of the job. If you are less qualified than your peers, emphasise what your work experience has taught you.

**Some believe that you'll only get interviewed if you match the job description exactly.** Organisations some-times want to buy in very specific experience, but they are often also interested in potential, and sometimes look for expertise acquired in other sectors. Three things may get you into an interview if you are a career shifter – enthusiastic interest in the sector, real knowledge of the job, and the ability to show how your skills and experience can add value, even if your experience doesn't obviously match.

**You'll have to retrain to change career.** Another powerful myth – believing that you will have to put your career on hold and borrow money to retrain. Unless you are moving into something highly specialised with prescribed entry qualifications, you can probably enter a new sector and then pick up key skills and experience as you go along. Mistrust absolutes: if you're told that certain qualifications are vital, seek people who have discovered backdoor routes.

Here's something you'll hear a lot: **Apply for as many jobs as you can.** Playing the job search lottery has one major consequence you haven't factored in – *disappointment*. Every rejection, or zero response, knocks you back. Applying for roles where you're a poor match wastes an employer's time and sets you up for repeated failure. How much time do you think a busy manager will give to a speculative CV with no obvious connection to the company's needs? Save your energy – make well-researched applications for roles where you're a credible candidate. Speculative approaches can give you access to the hidden job market, but only if they are extremely well targeted and followed up by personal contact.

**You need to get out there and SELL yourself.** How many times have you heard that? Over-selling can easily make you sound inauthentic, or desperate. Don't try to fake it or present yourself as a superhero, but present the best version of yourself, with clear supporting evidence. This idea is linked to another urban myth: **only pushy people network**

**effectively.** Networking works for everyone as long as they do it openly, honestly, and in a style that feels natural. Start by asking great questions and describing what really interests you (see Chapter 15, and also my book *The Success Code*).

Finally, there are a host of other **job-hunting myths** to stop you in your tracks: **A job's a job. Think of the money. Good jobs are hard to find.** Okay, red card. Go back to Chapter 1. Do not pass Go. Do not collect £200.

## Multi-channel job searching

There are many channels which will take you closer to jobs – job boards, company web sites, recruitment agencies, social media, direct approaches to organisations, headhunting, and word-of-mouth recruiting. Candidates often rely on just one or two channels, and many prefer to rely on using online job boards. This is rather like deciding that whatever your health problem, your only remedy is aspirin. Today's job market is complicated, with lots of distractions and dead ends. As this chapter will reveal, employers are shifting behaviours and recruiting using methods which cost little. To succeed, you need to operate using all channels, *not just the channels you prefer.*

Combining job search methods increases their power. This multi-channel approach doesn't ignore online activity, but ensures it takes up no more time than it deserves. Get it right, and you will consciously target the hidden job market and stand out from the crowd.

### How to conduct a multi-channel job search

- Research work sectors, and build up a list of target organisations.
- Undertake temporary or project work that increases your visibility to decision-makers.

- Scrutinise job advertisements to identify likely employers and useful agencies.
- Monitor internal job boards operated by employers.
- Conduct information interviews (see Chapter 15) to deepen your understanding of sectors, while improving your contacts and visibility.
- Be visible and distinctive on social media. Use LinkedIn to reach out to informative and supportive new contacts (see Chapter 14).
- Follow up recommendations to talk to people and organisations, but do your homework first.
- Ask for meetings with people who are at the heart of great networks.
- Talk to recruitment consultants who regularly advertise jobs in your target sectors.
- Approach companies in your chosen sectors on a speculative basis. Write a cover letter matching four or five of your key areas of experience to the employer's needs.
- Submit carefully matched applications in response to interesting vacancies.

## How employers prefer to find new staff

Here's some information that probably in itself justifies the cover price of this book.

UK government research statistics analyse the way employers fill vacancies. Some methods are paid for – using employment agencies, for example, or paid-for job advertisements. Other, 'internal' channels cost little or nothing – job postings on the organisations' own websites or social media pages, for example. However, one free 'internal' method stands out in terms of popularity: word of mouth or personal recommendation.

The *Employer Perspectives Survey 2016* was published in June 2017 by IFF Research for the Department for Education. The report looks at the way employers use both external and internal resources to recruit new staff. According to the report, 81% of employers used 'multiple methods of recruitment'. 'External' resources often require expenditure – for example, published vacancies, job boards, or using staffing agencies. Some external resources are free, for example, Jobcentres or university careers services. However, the report shows how employers use 'internal' resources extensively. These include times when an employer advertises vacancies on its own website or through its own social media channels, but the most important 'internal' resources are almost entirely free of charge. The two most common channels in this category are 'word of mouth' and 'personal recommendations'.

The report notes that 79% of employers used word of mouth or personal recommendation, adding that 'approaching three in ten . . . employers *only* used internal resources to recruit' (emphasis added). Other 'internal' methods were also popular – 'placing adverts on their website (54%) and using social media (46%)'. A smaller proportion, 44%, used 'another form of paid-for recruitment service, including the press' (www.gov.uk/government/publications/employer-perspectives-survey-2016).

A comparison with previous surveys suggests that employers are increasingly using word of mouth or personal recommendations to find new staff. Smaller establishments and new businesses tend to rely heavily on this method. Some sectors, notably construction (85% of employers), use word of mouth almost exclusively. It is clear that personal connections play an important role in recruitment, with word-of-mouth connections as well as personal recommendations from family, friends or colleagues becoming an increasingly important method of recruitment.

## Employer safety habits

Building on what we know about employer recruitment methods, it's clear that employers and job seekers use totally opposite strategies, and see risk very differently. We will look at each employer strategy in detail below.

### *Employers draw on personal connections*

Organisations like to hire people they already know. If they can't find what they are looking for internally, they find others close by who feel 'almost family'. Organisations like the security of new workers whose work performance can be predicted.

Some candidates feel this is about hiring through personal connections, but the simple fact is that organisations prefer known contacts to strangers. It's all about visibility. You might be recommended through a networking contact (or someone you met at an information interview). You may be known because you've worked with the organisation before. You might be visible because several people in a sector have mentioned your name.

### *Employers seek word-of-mouth recommendations*

If an employer doesn't already know someone, they don't rush to the market. They ask around. It's all about recommendation. Look around you. Who admires what you do and would be happy to recommend you to others? Have you enlisted help from these people as career coaches, dummy interviewers, idea factories? Look more closely at family, friends, local contacts – anyone is good at sharing information. Life has its natural match-makers and fixers, and they love to be known for their contacts and good judgement.

**How employers and candidates see risk differently**

| Perceived risk level for candidates | Employer method of attracting candidates to a vacancy | Perceived risk level for employers |
|---|---|---|
| High | 1. Personal connections<br>2. Word-of-mouth recommendations | Low |
| Medium | 3. Using external recruiters<br>4. Finding people using social media<br>5. Unsolicited approaches from candidates | Medium |
| Low | 6. Advertising the job on the company website<br>7. Advertising the job externally | High |

## *Employers use external recruiters*

Sometimes organisations work closely with recruitment consultancies. These become important intermediaries. Their role is to fill the job, not help you with your career anxieties. Working with external recruiters has positive and negative aspects for job hunters (see later in this chapter).

### Employers seek recommendations and candidates via social media

If an organisation can't find the right person through personal networks, it often reaches out via social media. Sometimes recruiters will approach you directly because your LinkedIn profile lists relevant skills or organisation names. At other times social media can alert you to the fact that an organisation is interested in meeting the right people.

Word of mouth happens in ways that are difficult to track. A friend may see a Tweet and mention it over coffee. You might reach out via LinkedIn and make a speculative phone call, or go through a formal recruitment process. Informal and formal, electronic and human – all becomes blurred. However, an employer is really asking, 'who do we know who knows someone worth talking to?'

How do you become a known quantity like this? Shine. Get to be good at your job and let others know it. Write articles or circulate good ideas. Keep an updated record of your achievements.

### Employers receive unsolicited approaches from candidates

Unsolicited applications get a bad press from candidates who send standard, untailored CVs at random to hundreds of employers. If an employer has spent time informally broadcasting a vacancy, incoming expressions of interest are welcome. If an employer is anticipating future needs, they will also be interested to hear from suitable candidates.

This does *not* mean emailing CVs on a 'spray and pray' basis. Speculative approaches need to be highly targeted, matching organisational needs. They work even better if you make a personal approach rather than relying on a cold email.

### Employers advertise the job on their own website and social media pages

If an organisation puts a vacancy on its own site, it's speaking to multiple audiences – current staff, those following the organisation online, and people well-connected enough to be directed towards roles through tip-offs and recommendations. Apply extremely carefully, matching your evidence against the job's key requirements.

### Employers advertise roles externally

By the time an organisation decides to advertise a role, employer risk increases. The floodgates will now open. As Chapter 1 outlines, job advertisements are often *candidate magnets* – all kinds of people apply, including many who are unsuitable. Many applications look undifferentiated – 'vanilla'. Your chances of being shortlisted are low, even if your skills are excellent, and yet many people put most of their time into chasing advertised roles. It's fairly passive: you fill in a form or submit a CV and then pat yourself on the back for a good day's work.

Someone relatively junior may be short listing, probably into three piles: 'No', 'Possible', and 'Yes'. In a competitive market, the 'Possible' tray is dispensed with. Work hard to get that initial 'Yes'. In your covering letter, use half a dozen bullet points to show you're a good match. Remember that reading a CV is a dull chore for HR professionals, and a frustrating distraction for line managers. Make your CV count (see my book *Knockout CV,* and also Appendix 2 in this book).

## Working more productively with recruitment consultants

Recruitment consultancies find candidates to fill jobs for employers. Agencies range from high-street operations to executive search consultancies, or 'headhunters'. Although recruitment consultants keep candidate databases, they are largely vacancy-driven. They are most interested if you fit a vacancy that needs filling immediately.

The main advantage of recruitment consultants is their closeness to decision-makers gives them the leverage to persuade an employer to see candidates – and issue job offers – quickly. Aim to establish contact with about 12–15 agencies that frequently fill the kinds of roles you are seeking. You will also be asked to register, sometimes online, but remember that recruiters are people-oriented, so establish a relationship. This works best by meeting face-to-face. Find the names of individual consultants handling the roles you're interested in. Send a speculative email with your CV. Phone a couple of days later and ask for the opportunity to meet the consultant. Recruitment consultants like to be valued for their industry knowledge, and often agree to meet if they feel they can learn something about the organisations you've worked in.

Recruitment consultants have a good feel for the market and can provide sound feedback about how employers will react to your CV. Less professional agencies will flatter you when you register and never come back to you. Some don't know as much as they should about a job, and some will be reluctant to put you forward if you haven't done a similar role in the past.

A good recruitment consultant will also tell you what you are worth in the marketplace, and what hurdles you will have to jump if you want to change sector. Many recruitment consultants have strong views about CV construction. Don't ask, 'what do you think of my CV?'. Do ask, *'what does my CV say to you?'* Listen to the story coming back at you. If you recognise and like what you hear, your CV is working well enough.

**Working with executive recruiters, by Joëlle Warren**

*The following no-nonsense tips from an executive recruiter reveal how you establish and build good relationships with recruitment consultancies.*

1.  Focus on being exceptionally good at your job and making a positive impact. Good headhunters will then find you – but make yourself visible to them so that they can. Writing articles, speaking at conferences, and receiving industry awards all help.
2.  Identify recruiters who specialise in your industry/function and build a relationship before you're in job search mode by using your network to gain introductions and being helpful and considered when you're asked for recommendations; then prioritise who you want to stay in touch with. Don't forget you are divulging confidential information about yourself and potentially your employer, so do your homework around the recruitment company's reputation, expertise, values, and ethics. Do they feel a good match?
3.  Strategically target the consultant within a firm who specialises in your function or sector. This individual should facilitate connections to colleagues who might be pertinent to you – but you may need to ask them, particularly if you are open to changing

sectors. Recruiters have a habit of putting you in a box, so it's better if you choose the box (or boxes) you want to be in. It is not necessary to contact multiple individuals within the same firm.

4. In terms of cold-calling a headhunter, email is still preferable to a phone call as a first introduction due to the heavy volumes headhunters receive, since it gives a quick impression of you and allows the headhunter to circulate your credentials among their colleagues and enter them into their global databases. The headhunter will immediately look for what is unusual or uniquely differentiating in your CV, so it's important you include quantitative information such as the size of the jobs you have held, organisations for which you have worked, the number of people you have managed, and results/ profits for which you have been accountable.

5. The email accompanying your CV should give a quick snapshot of your career drivers: title, geography, compensation, and the types of opportunities you are interested in. If you do send a cut-and-paste email to a variety of headhunters, make sure it's personalised and all the typeface is in the same size and font!

6. Avoid 'spamming' headhunters with multiple unso-licited emails each week or phoning them several times in a day, as these efforts may backfire.

7. Be transparent without being overly self-promotional during any phone or in-person meeting with a repre-sentative from a search firm. Do not make claims that will not stand up to rigorous background and reference checking – the headhunter's duty of care to their clients necessitates a reasonably thorough investigation of candidates, and they will quickly discover anything that is fabricated or exaggerated.

8. Assess opportunities proffered by headhunters realistically. Do not feign interest in a job that you are not intending to follow through on simply to get face-time with a recruiter – it will waste their time and not position you as a serious candidate.
9. When meeting the recruitment consultant, always have in the back of your mind that first impressions count: be prepared, be punctual, be smart, don't be afraid to 'use' the headhunter – ask for honest feedback on interview performance.
10. Once you've had a positive meeting or telephone call, ask the headhunter for their preferred method of staying in touch – phone or email – and how often.
11. Demonstrate that you 'know how the system works' by offering to help with open assignments; enhance your reputation with the headhunter by referring friends and colleagues that you hold in high regard (assuming they're at the right level and in a relevant sector) to them.
12. Be open with the headhunter about which firms you are trying to establish a relationship with – ask if there is any one they would personally recommend. Share openly and honestly how the rest of your job search is going.

**Joëlle Warren, Executive Chair,**
**Warren Partners**

## The hidden job market

Having looked at employer recruitment methods and preferences, you may be coming to a conclusion: chasing conventionally advertised jobs, particularly those on online job boards, may not always be the best use of your time and energy.

A substantial proportion of jobs are not advertised. This is the hidden job market. A few job hunters are unaware of it; many don't know how to break into it. If you want to slow down your job search and limit your options (maybe somebody is paying you to fail?), then act on the negative job myths set out above and limit your job search to advertised positions. You'll miss out on most newly created jobs, all positions filled by word of mouth, and most jobs with small, energetic companies. You'll miss out on all those companies that are just on the edge of thinking about creating a new job. You'll never have a chance to be recommended by a friend or colleague.

We've seen how employers are increasingly relying on word of mouth to find talent. This trend looks set to continue – employers are keen to harness a range of free and cost-effective methods, including social media, but they frequently fall back on the question, 'who do we know?'

We've looked at employer preferences. Any attempt to research the channels which work best for job seekers is problematic, since in an age of instant communication, channels overlap. We know that some people get roles through existing or new personal connections – usually by knowing someone in the organisation. We also know from evidence that men find this method of job searching easier than women. Sometimes, personal connections happen by chance or instinct; at other times, candidates sharpen their interpersonal skills to get in front of people with the right influence.

International studies point to a rule of thirds – in recent decades, on average about a third of all jobs have been filled by word of mouth. The employer research discussed earlier in this chapter suggests that this proportion may be increasing significantly. Similarly, about a third of job seekers also find jobs using word of mouth. However, be aware that research data relates to *all* jobs, from entry level upwards. As soon as you look at highly skilled, managerial or professional roles, or jobs in niche sectors, the percentage of those who find work through personal connections increases. In some sectors, most senior roles are never advertised.

There are as many urban myths about the unadvertised market as there are job sites. The hidden job market seems confusing, largely because so much goes on under the radar. Communication channels blur and overlap. People hear about organisations that are interested in talking to candidates – through conversations over coffee, Twitter, news feeds, from other candidates.

What's running through your head right now? *You're going to tell me the answer is networking.* Well, in a way – your way. Find out more in Chapter 15.

### 'Open' may still be 'hidden'

If you think that the only fair way of finding a job is to throw your hat in the ring alongside other candidates, be warned. 'Unhidden' jobs may not be as 'open' as they look. Someone may already be considered a good fit for a role, and may even have been promised it informally. There may be an internal candidate who everyone (apart from you) knows is in line for the job. Advertised positions can also have a hidden flavour: favoured candidates are told that a job is about to be advertised and invited to apply – so they are already on the shortlist. This happens more often than you think. Sometimes, employers have a preferred candidate already but go to the market to find benchmarks for comparison.

Jobs, therefore, are filled every day without the market having any sense that a vacancy ever existed. This feature of the marketplace can take a lot of stress out of job hunting. If you meet an organisation and they like you, a job may be created around you. If an employer finds you through personal connections and recommendations (see above), you can easily end up in a shortlist of one. It's all about being spotted, and becoming a known quantity.

### Job seeking: the ADEPT model

Here's a model which summarises the whole process of career transition:

**A – Adjusting to change.** The first stage covers much of the work of this book: your mindset, constraints, and understanding what gets in the way of finding a job you love. Look at what you are putting in the way of your own progress, and then look hard at what you need to start doing to make change happen. How are you going to overcome difficulties talking about your past, or difficulties making change happen in a tight market?

This phase is about getting your mindset right, and starting to work on yourself, and also with others. Plan now to deal with setbacks and rejection, and recruit supportive friends to help keep your spirits up during the process.

**D – Discovering yourself.** Catalogue your skills, strengths, and personal qualities. These will become the ingredients of your marketing message. You don't need to be over analytical, just get a really strong sense of what you are good at, where you have achieved something, and what you have to offer a new employer. Work through the relevant exercises in this book and learn to talk about yourself.

**E – Exploring what's out there.** Before long you'll be itching to get to grips with something even more tangible, so the exploring stage means finding out what's really out there. Put research before job search: follow your curiosity and get information from real people holding down real jobs, not second-hand information. Become hungry for new discoveries and connections. Your research should be focused on conversations, not the internet, to ensure that you learn quickly and get yourself remembered in the process.

**P – Pitching your message.** Now is the time to decide on the message you're going to communicate, in your CV, at interview, and in every conversation you have about career change. To do this you need to know (a) what you are selling and (b) who you are selling to. Next you need a quick summary in under two minutes that captures your background, what you have to offer, and what you're looking for. Test your message out for impact by rehearsing it with anyone with hiring experience, then try it out on people you are comfortable talking to. Once you feel it is working reasonably well, you can pitch it at useful contacts and then decision-makers.

Rehearse your two-breath message (see p. 218), and plan short, positive **Safety Zone Responses** (see p. 247) to back up your main pitch.

**T – Targeting.** Set targets for your job search. Decide how many people you are going to talk to each week and how many organisations you will approach, and keep a log to make sure your activity levels are maintained. Use all elements in a multi-strategy job search, particularly direct, speculative approaches to companies who are not advertising, and both face-to-face and online networking.

**A**djusting to change
What's the problem?
What's missing in your career?
What changes in your life are you trying to come to terms with?

**D**iscovering yourself
You, your skills
Your personality
Your goals
Your choices

**E**xploring what's out there
Researching potential fields/the marketplace

**P**itching your message
Everything that communicates who you are and what you are looking for

**T**argeting
Organisations that may be a great match for your skills and experience

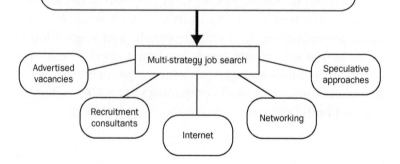

## 'Must do' list

✓ Base your job search on reality, not urban myths.
✓ Avoid the rookie mistakes many people make in the first few months of job searching.
✓ Spend more time and energy on the activities that shorten your job search and protect your confidence level.
✓ Take account of employer risk aversion in your job search strategy.
✓ Use a multi-channel strategy to unlock the hidden job market.
✓ Start your networking today – think of two positive-minded friends you can approach for encouragement and ideas.

# 14

# Hunting and connecting online

'Live in fragments no longer. Only connect . . .'
**E.M. Forster, *Howards End***

*This chapter looks at:*

- The value, and necessity, of having an online presence
- How to use social media as part of an active networking plan
- The classic errors people make online
- Online job searching.

## Why the internet may not save your career

In the twenty-first century, job seekers make the same mistakes career changers made in the 1980s and 1990s. We're still essentially passive, waiting for the right opportunity to come along, waiting for the phone to ring, waiting for someone else to take control of our career. Before mobile phones, job hunters stayed home in case the phone rang. Now we sit at our desks and pray to St Google.

A large proportion of job seekers focus most on one activity: searching online. Why do so many people believe this is the quickest and best way to find a job? First, it's easy – job sites are readily accessible from hand-held devices. Second, sitting in front of a screen uploading your

CV to job boards *feels* productive. Even more importantly, it *looks like work.*

Research published by the Boston Consulting Group in 2016 claimed that UK job hunters believed the most effective method for finding a job was 'internet job sites'. The second most common method was 'referral from family and friends'. According to social media strategist Ruth Winden, 'Employee referrals are the fastest growing way of finding job opportunities – employer research suggests that the quality of candidates found this way is higher, they become productive more quickly, and retention rates are improved.' Word-of-mouth recruitment is also obviously cheaper for employers. Therefore, getting to know people in target organisations matters.

Some years ago, I helped out at a job workshop in the San Francisco Bay area. It was salutary to see that even in a relatively buoyant, hi-tech economy there were career changers expressing the same worries as job hunters everywhere. Local outplacement specialists had a rule: *Use your PC outside working hours. During the day, use shoe leather.* The reason is simple. The web is fantastic for research, reasonably good at firming up connections, but poor at opening doors for the first time. A Tweet is forgotten in seconds, an email in minutes, a phone call in about half an hour. However, a warm face to-face meeting (followed up by a thank-you note) can easily be remembered for over 12 months. So, don't get locked into electronic correspondence – turn initial approaches into direct (private, offline) messages and then actual conversations.

### Use job boards as a back-up system, not the main event

Job boards are useful, but it's tempting to rely on them too heavily. They are best used as part of a multi-strategy approach. Register with job boards that (a) handle enough traffic so that jobs relevant to you come up every week, or (b) specialise in sectors that interest you. Upload a good-quality electronic CV, and make sure you use key words that hirers are searching for. Be aware how applicant tracking software (ATS) is being used to screen applications. Research the key words that recruiters search for using the tracking software; include these words in any text that describes you, including online profiles.

Use job boards in unconventional ways, too. They enable you to identify hiring organisations, and the recruitment consultancies searching for talent on their behalf. You can search by specialism, sector, role title or by location to find organisations on your doorstep. Job postings reveal job titles as well as the language employers are using to describe top performers and key skills.

Don't ignore company websites, where you will come across jobs not advertised elsewhere. Large employers often invest a great deal in creating sophisticated career pages on their sites because they want to have direct contact with candidates.

**Misunderstanding online job hunting, by Ruth Winden**

Job seekers often rely too much on the internet to find a new position: posting their CVs onto large CV banks in the hope that a recruiter will find them; searching online for job openings day in, day out; submitting untailored applications and then wondering why they never get a response.

I recommend limiting the time you spend online and having a clear four-step strategy:

1. Research companies to create a selective target list of suitable employers.
2. Set up relevant job alerts on aggregate job boards such as indeed.co.uk and glassdoor.co.uk, as well as industry-specific niche job boards.
3. Use social media to nurture and grow connections, raise visibility and credibility with recruiters and hiring managers (see material on LinkedIn below).
4. Follow companies and individuals, share their posts (if relevant to your networks) and contribute to the conversation with quality comments. Do this well, and you will get on their radar in the best possible way. Recruiters can search amongst candidates who follow the companies they are recruiting for, and regard such followers as 'warm contacts', as they have already expressed their interest in an employer, provided they are suitable candidates. Do the same wherever your industry, target employers and recruiters congregate – on social media or other sites (ranging from GitHub to Mumsnet).

**Ruth Winden, social media strategist & career coach (careersenhanced.com)**

## How using social media can give you an edge

While some are happy to follow and update Twitter all day, others fail to see the point, or just see an embarrassing over-supply of trivial information. There are two main reasons you may discover that social media can make a difference.

The first reason is about *visibility*. How are people going to find you? When your name comes up in conversation, hirers look you up on social media. Will they find you online? Does your online profile make sense to a target employer?

Visibility leads to *recommendation*. When someone looks at your profile, which parts of it will encourage someone to recommend you? This is more important today because of the ever-increasing popularity of employee referrals, where staff are incentivised for introducing candidates to a business.

The second reason is about *people*. Making a big life change is about relationships: making connections with people who will provide you with ideas, information, referrals – and encouragement. Your relationship needs to be with people, not with Google, but the best way to find and contact the right people now is to join (or even create) online networks.

Ignoring these readily accessible, free resources slows down progress, closes doors, and firmly suggests you have no interest in modern communication tools.

### Using social media to underpin your job search

It's no use hoping someone will find you online by chance. You need a shop window that is easy to find and clearly sets out what you do. LinkedIn is an ideal tool for this purpose, as it's widely used, easy to manage, and gives you a great deal of freedom about how you present information. LinkedIn now offers three facilities: short updates, longer form content like a blog piece, and video. The last two are really helpful to job hunters because they allow different ways of showcasing your interest and your evidence. A personal blog space can often be very important because it's one of the few online spaces where you have total control over content.

Look at your online profile with a critical eye. Is your main focus of work clear, at a glance? Are you including the right keywords in your headline, summary, and work experience sections, so interested parties will find you? Are you supporting your professional achievements with facts and evidence? Evidence might include videos of presentations, blog posts, articles you were quoted in, photos, certifications, and any proof of your professional accomplishments. With diminishing trust in online information, it is more important than ever to back up what you claim.

Get someone to look at your online information. Ask them to summarise what they see. LinkedIn users have two ways of getting strapline messages across. The first is a job title (or a summary phrase that captures your role or expertise). This is very important, as it's usually taken as an indication of what you want to do next. Does this opening information put you into a useful box? Second, you have a 'status bar', which is essentially a quick update of what you are doing, often linked to your Twitter account.

Don't confuse business with letting your hair down. If you want to look like a serious, committed candidate, don't fill online space with updates on your cat, your love life or favourite recipes. Use a separate, friends-only Facebook account for that. Think about how much information you really want to be spread across the web. If you live on the wild side, make sure that your on-screen confessions, conversations, and photographs are visible only to trusted friends. Many employers and recruiters use the internet for background checking. If you insist on posting photographs of yourself in a state of undress or inebriation, you might as well bring them with you to the job interview – it's called *public domain* for a reason.

## Look for people, not jobs

If you want to change career by moving into a new sector, then focus on the one activity that is likely to make the biggest difference: *contact with other people.* You'll often hear the suggestion, 'it's not what you know, it's *who* you know, and who knows you'. However, as Chapter 15 will reveal, this idea is often used as a great excuse not to find anyone to get to know. The great advantage of social media is that you can make more contacts at greater speed than any previous generation. Contact details update themselves without you needing to keep records, and you can also follow people without being directly connected to them.

Although your ultimate aim is to get face-to-face meetings, you have to find some means of initial contact. Fortunately, most of the people you need to reach can be contacted online. An email out of the blue is likely to be ignored, so how do you use electronic communication to reach decision-makers?

Focus on an organisation that interests you. Look for named individuals – decision-makers with real needs. Follow their blog and Twitter accounts; find out what interests them. Ruth Winden's advice: 'Be helpful, answer questions, share postings you find worth sharing with your community, engage. Being genuinely interested in other professionals and their projects will get you noticed and can be a great way to start a conversation, develop a relationship based on common interests, and eventually open doors. Just remember that all good relationships take time to develop, so do not wait until you are in a job search situation.'

Once you know something about a decision-maker, you can consider a direct approach. Before you do so, ask yourself: 'Is there any approach method available other than email?' Ask around: who do you know who works in your target organisation, or has worked there in some capacity, including a consultant or supplier? Referral from an existing employee will always get you in the door quickest. Use LinkedIn to spot people who are connected to someone in or near your target organisation. If you find someone you know who has a connection, pick up the phone and ask for an introduction. If that really isn't possible, make your own direct approach by email. When you do so, remember the principles of any job search letter: keep it short and focused, and spell out just two or three reasons why that person might want to see you. You're after a face-to-face meeting at this stage, not a job offer.

### How to manage your online presence if you are between jobs

People are often unsure what to say online if they are unemployed. Don't use LinkedIn to broadcast the fact that you are out of work. Hirers and recruiters use LinkedIn to find experience, not availability. Don't waste the opportunities it presents by using your status bar to say that you are seeking work or still unemployed. Avoid statements such as 'have been looking for some time now' or 'will consider anything'. You wouldn't put that in a CV, so don't make it part of your LinkedIn profile.

Quirky phrases like 'looking for next great opportunity!' or the rather twee 'in the enviable position of being available to assist a new employer' sound like mild desperation. Your message is your expertise, not your empty diary. A phrase such as 'Qualified procurement specialist' is great – condensing experience and credibility into three words. You may, however, get away with a clear, focused, and unemotional statement, such as 'seeking full-time employment as an HR Manager in the East Midlands area'. Questions of tone are difficult to get right – ask the opinion of someone you trust to give you objective advice *before* you publish any statement of this kind.

Keep things updated: don't leave your LinkedIn page dormant with no updates for several months, or people will assume you have found a position or lost interest. Ruth Winden suggests: 'Signal to recruiters you are open for job opportunities on the "Career Interest" tab, under the "Job Search" tab. Here you can define your job targets – from type of employer to skills and salary range, in confidence. This information is only accessible to recruiters and their specific software. Remember to refresh this setting every 6 weeks.'

It's sometimes hard to think of updates when your only message is, 'I'm still here and still looking.' Update your status bar with updates on the things you are researching, and the things you want to know more about.

Think about ways of keeping your message varied and interesting. Make sure your online profile reveals activity, showing you're doing something for yourself rather than waiting for the market to come to you. Demonstrate enthusiasm, for example: 'Reading everything I can get my hands on about healthcare reform . . .', or 'Just watching a fascinating presentation on green building construction'. Show not just your interest, but the fact that you are up to date. Put in live links to websites, blogs, videos, and podcasts so that readers can learn more about the things that have inspired you. Bookmark interesting pages so you can send out recommendations on a drip-feed basis – one a day, for example, rather than a whole burst in one evening.

Since recruiters often find candidates this way, it's a good idea to include your email address and perhaps also a phone number on LinkedIn. Recruiters are always working against the clock and will often work with the candidates they can reach quickest.

**LinkedIn: Top 15 tips for job searchers, by Julian Childs**

1. Think of your LinkedIn profile as a next step towards intimacy with someone who has just read your formal CV – consistent but more informative

so that a reader can feel they know you a little better or more personally from considering it.

2. If LinkedIn is a high street, then your profile is like an individual shop from which you are selling expertise and experience services under your personal brand. Use your first name and surname as simply as possible and in the same format as on your CV, business card, email address and signatures. Variations confuse.

3. Promote your business pitch succinctly next to your name and make it as unique as possible. Mine currently reads 'Careers Expert + LinkedIn Marketer + International Connector + Talent Catalyst + Start-Up Advisor', and at the time of writing is the only one out of 530 million users in more than 200 countries and territories listed on LinkedIn, compared with about 33,000 people who describe themselves simply as 'Career Coach'.

4. Upload a pleasant, friendly, approachable, smart, and professional looking photo of yourself. Colour or black and white is fine but do not use holiday snaps, arty poses, cartoons, symbols, company logos or avatars.

5. Edit the URL that LinkedIn allocates to you so that it mirrors your name and personal brand. Then copy this detail on your business card, email signature, and CV to encourage people to visit your profile.

6. The 'Summary' section of your profile allows you to craft, test, and communicate a powerful elevator pitch. Use the 'Specialties' sub-section to list your areas of expertise and interest for search engines.

7. Write a brief, positively worded description of your responsibilities and achievements in each position along your career path and enhance these with strong recommendations.

8. Join and follow alumni groups for everywhere you have studied, as well as the largest and most relevant LinkedIn groups in every industry or professional sector that you wish to explore. Monitor these daily for jobs and influential contacts, and participate in group discussions to feed your expertise and interview prowess.

9. Link the 'Update' box to your Twitter account and use it occasionally to share your views, opinions, inspirational quotes or authoritative articles sourced for relevance from your LinkedIn home page or credible external sources. You can also promote your involvement or attendance at industry events here and, similarly, more and more people are using this facility to upload photos or short punchy videos. Create content as well as sharing it.

10. Frequency of decent quality content is the name of the game and done well, regular updates can make you look expert and raise your profile. By the same token, be mindful and careful not to look silly by posting inaccurately, clumsily, inappropriately or too often.

11. Identify people you would like to connect with and personalise your template invitation message to introduce and contextualise your interest. If you don't already know them, perhaps start by following their activity for a few days and comment intelligently in the discussion threads under their posts to get onto their radar and seed your later approach.

12. Research target companies via the search bar, then 'Follow' for news and contacts in those you want to target. Similarly, join the largest relevant special interest 'Groups' and participate tactically in their discussions, as well as monitoring for vacancies posted there.

13. Using the search bar, enter an ideal job title and company to identify relevant vacancies. Then, see if you already have – or could readily create – connections inside the target business to chat with before you apply. This could trigger a personal referral that effectively puts you ahead of any lesser known candidates being considered for the job.

14. Use the search bar to reveal people with your ideal job title, organisation, and location. Their profiles will indicate how they got there and also identify any friends in common. Ask your mutual acquaintance to introduce you, then arrange an informational interview perhaps using the REVEAL method outlined in this book. This can be brilliant for establishing useful allies inside target organisations and win you fast access to the elusive unadvertised job market.

15. LinkedIn's 'Help Center' page (with US spelling!) can answer most questions about LinkedIn and typing 'use LinkedIn to . . .' on YouTube will show you many more tricks too.

**Julian Childs, career coach and business advisor (www.linkedin.com/in/julianchilds)**

### Think about who will be following you

To follow you, people need to find your profile on social media. People want to know they've found the right person, so make sure you include up-to-date information about your location, specialisms, and work history. Your page should show that you are following relevant online discussion groups and professional bodies.

Posting negative information will slow you down like a dead weight. When posting online, don't say anything negative about yourself, past employers or bosses, or any of the organisations or recruitment consultancies you've had contact with in your job search.

## Can you get a job in 280 characters?

Some people believe you need thousands of followers to make an impact on Twitter, but even with a few followers you can start to make an impact. To use Twitter for job searching, set up an account specially for the purpose. Twitter once had great novelty as a job search tool but now competes with Instagram, SnapChat, and even Pinterest. However, Twitter is still important. Some great job sites broadcast through Twitter. Also, many key decision-makers use it as a platform for their thinking. This provides big hints about organisational culture – executives are likely to be more conversational and less guarded on Twitter than in other outlets.

Before you follow anyone on Twitter, it's important that you have a completed profile that shows, at a glance, who you are. This means a very short biography that includes useful and relevant hashtags, a summary of your expertise, your approximate location, and a link to a site that recruiters can go to for more information (a blog or your LinkedIn profile).

Present a succinct, understandable picture of who you are and what you do: keep it clear and simple. Don't overlook the simplicity of Tweeting clear messages, such as 'just got laid off, looking for a #job in #HR', because that may be enough to attract offers.

Be consistent in your use of Twitter – become known for what you say and what you use the platform for, and stick to it.

**Top tips for using Twitter when #job hunting, by Matthias Feist**

In September 2018, Matthias Feist set himself the challenge of summing up his advice in 11 tweets, using the hashtag #HTGAJYL, reprinted below. His tips work on the assumption that you know basic twitter functions and terms such as 'hashtag', 'mention', and 'retweet/RT'. Over the last two years, Twitter has changed – foremost in the doubled character limit it allows. This enables more complex conversations. With it came the emergence of threads, multi-part tweets which act as microblog posts, allowing an author to address issues in more detail. Those threads sometimes span dozens of entries with multiple replies to each individual post. In this tradition, here is Matthias' thread. There are many tutorials available on the net. Find and share . . .

**Thread:**

1/11 tweets on using Twitter as a tool for #howgetajobyoulove, in support of @JohnLeesCareers new edition of How To Get A Job You Love #HTGAJYL. It's not sponsored content, but I will be in the book. I like John and his advice is #IMHO excellent.

2/11 Create a Twitter profile connected to your #LinkedIn (Facebook & YouTube) profile. Use the same picture and mission statement throughout for consistency. Put your Twitter name on your CV. Disable any settings that automatically tweet – be selective. #HTGAJYL

3/11 Follow target #employers, their followers, #job tweets, relevant bloggers and experts in the field. Following others brings you followers. Make sure they are real and don't spout only promotional or fake content. Curate your followers, block bots. Be choosy. #HTGAJYL

4/11 Use #LinkedIn to update Twitter not more than once a day. Never push all updates via LinkedIn, only work and audience relevant ones. Choose your message of the day wisely – always ask – what's of most value to my audience? #HTGAJYL

5/11 Tweet a lot, say about 5 times daily to keep a flow. Consider e.g. Hootsuite to manage multi-platform posts: E.g. five tweets, one to LinkedIn, some to your Facebook page. #HTGAJYL

6/11 Only tweet what you think is relevant to your audiences. Use #hashtags picked up in relevant discussions, e.g. #HTGAJYL. Twitter at its best is funny, a snappy comment, a funny (but relevant) animated gif or short video shows you are fun to work with.

7/11 If something good is not worth retweeting, like it. People react well to likes. Adding value to their #professional Twitter feed will be good PR for you and the people you follow. #HTGAJYL

8/11 Don't worry too much about your original content at first, focus on sharing and adding value to others. Your first own tweets will always suck a bit. Relax. Twitter is immediate and boring content will just flow away. Move on. Others will, too. #HTGAJYL

9/11 Find your own voice: Write like you're in a #job engaging with peers: talk about topics relevant to #employers in twitter chats. It is OK to sprinkle in your own, even political opinion. But never be rude or spread #fakenews. Never #mansplain. #HTGAJYL

10/11 The Offline world just about still rules the online world: go #networking and meet the people you tweet. Also, live-tweet from events, and follow speakers.

Even better, post pics; use Periscope to live stream and share your own YouTube videos. Visuals beat text every time. #HTGAJYL

11/11 Check interviewers' tweets in advance, quote or refer to them if appropriate. They will check you in advance, you can do the same. Follow speakers, but don't be creepy. Never say anything you wouldn't say in front of other people and to their faces. #HTGAJYL

**@matthias_feist – Matthias Feist works in employability, enterprise, and alumni relations for Regent's University London and he is the previous Chair of PlaceNet, the Placements in Industry Network. He blogs at www.matthiasfeist.com**

## 'To do' list: Checklist for making the most of electronic media

| Protect your personal information online | |
|---|---|
| **WHY** | **HOW** |
| To avoid online fraud, you need to choose carefully what recruiters can see – and what they can't | Check your privacy settings regularly. Decide whether you want separate personal and professional social media profiles. Do not share your home address, birthday and personal details, including those of family |

| Selectively share personal information | |
|---|---|
| **WHY** | **HOW** |
| People connect with people they know, trust and like. | Decide what you are comfortable sharing about yourself. Even on |

| Trust comes from sharing common interests and personal information | LinkedIn, it doesn't all have to be 100% professional – but 'work related' still works best. Think updates and images of you volunteering, mentoring or coaching a sports team, or taking part in a charity fundraiser. Leave wise quotes, cute cat pictures, and jokes to less formal sites like Facebook or visual sites like Pinterest and Instagram |

| Create a compelling CV *and* LinkedIn profile | |
|---|---|
| **WHY** | **HOW** |
| You never know what people will see first | Both documents require compelling content – measurable achievements, plus the right keywords to get you noticed by online searches (LinkedIn) or Applicant Tracking Systems (CV). Make sure the opening section of your LinkedIn profile summarises your main skills, experience, and areas of focus |

| Make it easy for people to find you | |
|---|---|
| **WHY** | **HOW** |
| If you don't have an electronic footprint, you make it difficult for others to track you down – and people give up very quickly | Increase your chances of being approached for projects, networks, opportunities, and job openings. Use industry-specific keywords. If applicable, add in hashtags (#) in you bios, headlines, experience sections, and summaries. Find these keywords from job descriptions, industry publications, and leaders' profiles in your sector |

| Make it easy for people to reach out to you | |
|---|---|
| **WHY** | **HOW** |
| If someone wants to offer you something, they often want to communicate quickly and get a rapid response | Decide what access you are willing to give – email only? Landline or mobile? Avoid 'protecting' your Twitter account by forcing new followers to qualify themselves. Recruiters will ignore you if you play hard to get! Use the same name across all media platforms. Personalise URLs wherever possible, ideally with your name only |

| Create a positive visual impression | |
|---|---|
| **WHY** | **HOW** |
| If you don't include a photograph, your profile page is incomplete. In an age of 'fake news', people mistrust a great deal of material found online. A photograph helps confirm your profile is genuine | Use a bright, sharp photograph, in which your face fills the frame. Look professional but also friendly and approachable |

| Stand out from the crowd | |
|---|---|
| **WHY** | **HOW** |
| With hundreds of millions of online profiles, it's easy to be ignored. Don't try to appeal to everyone – focus on attracting the right contacts | Make sure you're noticed. Build a reputation for the type of information you share. Posts with images or videos get more attention than plain text. Add visuals (photo and header image on LinkedIn and Twitter). Use a consistent style of visuals to support your 'brand' |

| Include only relevant social media profiles on your CV, ideally as clickable hyperlinks ||
| WHY | HOW |
|---|---|
| Enabling readers to click through to your LinkedIn profile via a hyperlink on your CV helps recruiters find out even more compelling information about you than from your CV only | Copy and paste your LinkedIn hyperlink at the top of your CV with your contact details. If relevant to your target market, also add in your Twitter handle, Pinterest or Instagram account |

| Match the information that appears on your CV with your social media profiles ||
| WHY | HOW |
|---|---|
| If key dates and work information differ between your profiles and your CV, it creates doubt in your reader. And as they say – a confused mind doesn't buy! | Ensure basic information such as job titles, dates, and employer names are consistent. Include additional evidence a CV cannot provide – images, copies of certifications, presentations (via Slideshare), videos or links to articles you wrote or were quoted in, for industry publications or the press |

| Become a content producer or curator ||
| WHY | HOW |
|---|---|
| There's nothing better than being sought after, based on what people know and appreciate about you. By creating, sharing or curating information that serves your community of like-minded people, you | Select your ideal platform carefully, then use it to create, share, and respond to content relevant to you and your audience. Write a blog about a topic close to your heart; review books, products or events; recommend people and organisations. |

| | |
|---|---|
| (indirectly) highlight what you stand for and attract relevant opportunities | Be selective and strategic about what you share. Be consistent and patient. Your network will grow and opportunities will come your way – as long as your contributions are thoughtful, professional, and valuable |

| Make better use of the internet as a research tool | |
|---|---|
| **WHY** | **HOW** |
| Organisations detail vast amounts of information about what they are doing and the kinds of people they hope to attract, through job listings but also in news items, press releases and blogs from senior executives | Research organisations and work sectors. Follow key industry figures, trade associations, and professional bodies |

| Make a visual contribution to key discussions | |
|---|---|
| **WHY** | **HOW** |
| Showing that you follow key topics and can make an informed contribution to online discussion groups shows that you are serious about your current or target work sector | Keep abreast of developments – join relevant online discussion groups, asking good questions and making informative, relevant contributions |

| Check inputs and outputs | |
|---|---|
| **WHY** | **HOW** |
| Visibility needs to be maintained, and you need to know quickly if someone is trying to reach you | Have a plan for maintaining the quality and quantity of your online contributions. Keep on top of your inbox: check email and voicemail at least twice a day |

| Make connections! | |
|---|---|
| **WHY** | **HOW** |
| The more people you know, and they know you, the more opportunities will be open to you – provided that you invest time and effort in building lasting professional relationships. Online tools can connect you with people and opportunities well beyond your in-person networks – so use them wisely | On LinkedIn, always connect from someone's profile page so that you can personalise your invitation to connect. Give them a great reason to connect (rather than a bland 'I found you on the internet'), so they say 'yes' and you can start building that relationship. As soon as you are connected, continue the conversation, and aim to take it offline as soon as it feels comfortable to make a phone call or meet in person |

**Thanks to Ruth Winden for helping to produce this checklist.**

# Organised discovery: how people will move you forward

'The greatest obstacle to discovery is not ignorance –
it is the illusion of knowledge.' **Daniel J. Boorstin**

## The difficulty of doing the obvious

Chapter 13 investigated the hidden job market, showing
how it has grown and how job searching has become more
complicated.

In a first session I usually ask a new client which job
search method they think is most likely to bag them a job
offer. Even at this stage it seems obvious to most clients
that they will probably get quicker results through conversations and by making new connections. However, they are
reluctant to do anything that looks like networking.

Nearly all job searchers, whether graduates or executives, hate that word: *networking*. They say it feels uncomfortable, it's 'pushy', or 'it exploits people and loses you
friends'. Some are even more honest: 'it makes me feel
grubby . . . it makes me look desperate'. We should respect
these suspicions. Anyone who suggests you begin networking without addressing these issues is trying to get you to
buy a jacket that doesn't fit, isn't your colour, and is something you'll never wear after you take it home.

I've talked about initial conversations with clients. At the
end of a programme when someone has found a new role,

I have another question: 'If you find yourself on the job market again, what will you do differently next time?' The answer is nearly always, 'I would start talking to people earlier.' Not 'networking', you notice, but simply 'talking to people'.

There are lots of reasons for talking to people. When an exciting organisation phones you out of the blue, remind yourself that this apparently random event comes about as a result of your visibility. People find you because they hear about you. A huge part of job seeking is about being remembered and recommended. That doesn't happen immediately; first you need other kinds of conversation, asking for encouragement, ideas, information, and for introductions.

## Networking for softies

Connecting with new people is something we all do unconsciously. If you move to a new town and want to find a good childminder, dentist or plumber, you ask around. This is networking at its simplest. Networking has acquired a tarnished reputation – it either feels like taking advantage of people, or you imagine uncomfortable networking breakfasts where people talk at you and you're supposed to 'work the room', dishing out business cards. For most people, this kind of activity is as unproductive as it is dispiriting.

Stay with that simple idea: 'talking to people'. If you're a quiet person and find this daunting, be assured that you can do this in your own style. You don't have to deliver a glib 'elevator pitch' – you'll get perfectly good results by listening and asking great questions (for more on the way quieter people can make an impact, see my book *The Success Code.*)

Don't call it networking. Think of it as a way of locating helpful people, putting yourself in the path of interesting ideas and organisations. Think of it as making new friends.

Think of it as actively following your curiosity. Sometimes you'll be inspired, sometimes a door will open – and your challenge is that you don't know what will happen until you have the conversation.

Think of it, simply, as *meeting interesting people.* Keep to this relaxed agenda rather than constantly worrying about making a 'pitch'. Don't think, 'Who do I know that can get me into a job?'; instead, ask yourself: 'Who do I know that will have interesting answers to some of my questions?' Networking should never be about trashing friendships for the sake of a quick fix. Networks are *social* networks – they work best when we take a genuine interest in others. Be prepared to offer insights and information you've discovered. The process is about giving as much as taking – what 1950s careers writer Bernard Haldane described as a 'chain of helpfulness' and UK networking specialist Stuart Lindenfield calls '101 cappuccinos'.

Think of it as building a community of interest. Communities are not dependent on the total number of people they contain, but the connections between them. If four people are connected, that's 12 relationships. If you simply add one more person to the group, you get 20 relationships. As your personal web goes beyond ten, the number of possible interactions explodes. This shows the difference between mailing lists and interest groups. A mailing list may be 2000 separate, unconnected people. An interest group as small as 2000 can overturn national policy.

Be kind to yourself, and network like a true softie. Never ring cold, because that's a great way to set yourself up to fail. Start with people you know well – the people you can ring *without having to compose an opening statement in your head.* Start with people you can take out for coffee and say, 'this is going to come out all wrong, but can I try this out with you?' Ask anything you like, but *ask more than you tell.* Find out about the work they do, how they got into it, what overlaps exist between their world and yours. Thank your friend for their time, but don't say goodbye until you've asked the number one, all-time, breakthrough networking question:

*Who else should I be talking to?*

The best kind of networking is *not* directly focused on getting a job, but an indirect approach can generate more leads and ideas than you know what to do with. However, the conversation will always, at some point, come around to you. It might be 'What about you?' or 'What are you looking for?'

You need a quick summary. Note the word *quick*. Short, memorable, simple, upbeat – these are qualities that ensure that what you say is remembered.

## Your two-breath message

On average, you take 15,000 breaths a day. With just two of those breaths you can plant helpful ideas into your network, so that the right information comes up next time your name is mentioned. Work on your two-breath message. Two sentences, approximately – which sum you up and say where you're heading. A two-breath statement which sounds something like this:

*'I'm interested in finding a job that allows me to do A and B and C . . . in an organisation that's doing X and Y and Z.'*

Items A, B, and C are your motivated skills – the things you do best. Chapter 7 will identify them for you. X, Y, and Z describe things your ideal employer is doing. You might mention specific kinds of products, services, technology or approaches. You might talk about style (for example, hi-tech or cutting edge), culture (high quality or customer-focused) or the nature of the organisation (private, public, blue-chip, privately owned, etc.).

Listeners respond well to this kind of message – it's succinct, memorable, and energised. People respond to you more favourably than if you mention a job title, or if you ask for help identifying vacancies. The two-breath message should remind you of the TV show *Ready Steady Cook*: you dump the ingredients in front of someone, then ask for a good recipe to match. What people say in response are things like, 'you know, you really should talk to my friend Rashid . . .' or 'have you thought about talking to Acme Industries . . .' or, best of all, 'that sounds to me like . . .' – they identify a sector you haven't yet fallen across. This statement will help you in any situation where someone asks what you're looking for. You only get a few seconds of their attention, so leave them with a message they will remember.

## Degrees of separation

The theory of **six degrees of separation** was popularised by the US playwright John Guare. The idea is that you can reach anyone in the world in six jumps – or fewer. Person A leads you to B, B to C and so on. You can often begin by talking to someone who has only the vaguest connection to your target individual.

Here's an example. I regularly ask audiences, 'who's met someone who has been into space?' Twice in my life I came close to famous astronauts without even trying (Yuri Gagarin was Manchester's guest of honour when I was in my pram, and some 40 years later Neil Armstrong spoke at a venue ten minutes' walk from my office). Even though the first manned space mission was Gagarin's flight in April 1961, only a few hundred people have been up there. Yet, in my average audience, one person in 50 or so has talked to someone who has been in space. The first time I asked, a woman in the second row put her hand up, and told me that for her personally, her astronaut encounter was a life-changing conversation. Even the most extraordinary people are not that far away.

With large audiences I make sure that everyone in the room has a conversation with a stranger. It begins with a question: 'What are you looking for?' It's said that out of 300 people, half a dozen will sneak out at this point, claiming an urgent appointment. Sad because those 140-plus conversations are always useful, sometimes amazing. Later someone from the audience will find me and say, 'You know, I had a conversation today which may have changed my life.' The fact that it happens every time means that it just happens – you just need to keep asking.

## Information interviews

Information interviews are a form of networking, but much easier. An information interview is a way of organising your curiosity. It's an activity that works most of the time, is known about by most job seekers, but used by a tiny minority. A job interview is about persuading someone to offer you a job. An *information* interview is very different. Its main purpose is to unearth information – but it has many spin-off benefits.

You're more likely to need an information interview if you're thinking of a change of sector. Why? Because your map book is blank. You will have only a very limited idea of what exists, who's out there, and the kind of roles that need filling. When you're approaching organisations, you'll be guessing at the hot topics and buzzwords they use, and what makes them tick. You need to find out a great deal to become a credible candidate. Desk research will take you a long way, but you get there more quickly and with a lot of additional benefits by talking to people.

The idea is simple: find someone who knows about a work sector, and ask to see them for a short meeting, ideally face-to-face. As with any networking activity, start with someone you know well so the initial approach is easy. This isn't about selling yourself. Mostly, it's not about you at all. You'll be finding out about someone's role, their organisation, and the sector they work in. It's a low-stress process, because you're armed with a script (see below). Along the way you'll say something about why you're interested, and you'll gather the names of other people to talk to. It's not about telling, projecting, self-promotion – it's about absorbing information. This isn't pushy networking in disguise, and you're not trying to subversively obtain a job interview.

An information interview is a vital stepping stone to **discovery**. Conversations provide deep-level information – far more than you will ever glean from a website or company brochure. It's the inside story – what a job really feels like, and the realities of organisational culture. These interviews are also a key stage in improving your **visibility** – vital in the hidden job market (see Chapter 13).

### ☑ *Information benefits of information interviews*

- For a short but critical time, you put *research* before *job search*.
- You meet people in real jobs by moving from desk research to field research. You will learn about entry routes, sector trends, and organisational cultures.
- You understand the reality of jobs, so you can begin to decide if they will suit you.
- You spot the roles and sectors that match your skills and experience.
- You pick up clues that will help you match yourself to specific roles.
- You understand how top performers are described.
- You pick up the language you will need for job interviews.

### ☑ *Visibility benefits of information interviews*

- People remember you, especially if you see them face-to-face and thank them in writing afterwards.
- People remember your energy, your enthusiasm, your commitment, your reason for enquiring.
- The people you meet make connections on your behalf. Your name is mentioned when problems and opportunities come up.
- You learn enough information to sound like a credible candidate really committed to moving into a new sector.
- You are often talking to decision-makers, putting yourself on their radar for when problems or opportunities arise.
- You can actively plant information about you that you want others to remember.

### ☑ *Job-seeking benefits of information interviews*

- You learn more about jobs using this method than by applying randomly for roles or asking to be told if a vacancy comes up.
- You identify target organisations.
- When people understand what you're looking for, they can help you. If you're remembered, opportunities find you.
- You pick up insider language that allows you to convince people you really understand the sectors and organisations you're targeting.
- If you broadcast employable skills and knowledge via social media, you may get direct approaches from recruitment consultants.
- Your visibility may put you straight onto a short list, even if a job isn't advertised.
- *You fall over jobs*. It's true. Ironically, the indirect route, which is not focused on job search, often turns out to be the number one strategy for getting at the hidden job market.

- You discover jobs before they become vacancies. If they're not for you, tell other people in your network.

☑ **Confidence benefits of information interviews**

- You get to wear smart business clothes and visit places of work, which maintains your confidence levels in a job search.
- You get used to asking great questions and conveying memorable energy.
- You get used to talking about yourself, briefly.
- If you're changing sectors, you learn how to make your experience and skills sound relevant.
- Since you're tracking down people who share your vision of what work is about, you'll end up with new social contacts and friends.
- You leave people with a positive impression of you, and enough information to recommend you to others.

### Big and small asks

Information interviews work because they don't ask for too much. Think about how you react if someone rings you out of the blue and says, 'I'd appreciate your help in identifying jobs in your organisation.' You'd feel uncomfortable. You don't know the caller, so why would you recommend this person? The conversation would probably end there. Even requesting someone to look over your CV is a 'big ask' – it takes a lot of time to read a CV and give valid feedback.

A request for an information interview should not be a big ask. They work best when someone can deliver what you need with minimum effort. That's why you don't ask for career advice, or for someone to recommend you, or for tips on getting a job with the organisation. You ask about the person in front of you. People generally find it easy to talk about themselves and the job they do. If you make the conversation easy, people are usually prepared to pass you on to someone else.

## The REVEAL method

Information interviewing is a technique championed by both Richard Nelson Bolles and Daniel Porot. I am indebted to both of them for kick-starting my thinking and for inspiring me to design and market test the REVEAL model for information interviews.

REVEAL conversations are meetings you will arrange with key individuals who will love to talk about their industry sector. You will add to your personal knowledge, expand your network, and learn how jobs 'feel' from the inside. A meeting won't form a once-and-for-all career decision. It won't be a job interview – but sometimes will lead to one.

### Begin with people you know

There are tough ways of persuading people to see you. You could try working through the Yellow Pages. You could turn up at reception and ask for a meeting. Either might work, but they present an uphill struggle.

Get this step right and you never have to make a terrifying phone call. Start with the names of **three people** to approach. You will know them well, and they are easy to talk to. They might simply give you encouragement, information, or answers to some of your career questions. Start practising your REVEAL script. Ask how they got into their careers and what's happening in their work sectors. Ask, 'who should I talk to next?'

Can't think of anyone to talk to? Perhaps that's just your way of avoiding making a start. Even people who never think about networking usually have about 100 people within their immediate contact circle. If you're feeling a little more confident, you might start to reach out to people you're connected with through social media.

### Ask for a warm handover

Practise with people you know reasonably well, build your technique, and then get introduced to new contacts. Getting introduced means you never have to make a cold call. *At the beginning of every conversation,* say something like this: 'I'm hoping to speak to about a dozen people in this sector to gather a wide range of views.' Later, when you get to the end of the conversation and say, 'That was really helpful. Who else should I be talking to?', your colleague will probably already have thought of a name. Or several.

However, even if you hear names, you've only done half the job. A list of phone numbers or email addresses means you're back to cold calling. You have no choice but to begin by saying, 'You don't know me . . .'. It takes a huge amount of confidence to get past that difficult moment.

Your aim is to ask people to make a warm handover, so ask for what you need: 'I hate ringing people cold. Would you be kind enough to phone ahead for me, just to say who I am and why I'm interested?' One phone call (even one email) means that your next contact expects your call and knows what it's about. More importantly, they know enough to be assured that you're not selling something or asking for difficult favours. When you get in touch, your new contact knows why you're calling, and has picked up enough from the warm introduction to trust that you're not selling anything, and not after a 'big ask'. Often, all you have to mention is the name of the last person you met. This should be a good enough memory prompt ('Sure – Bill called me about you'). Draw on personal connections between one contact and the next ('Bill tells me you're a keen fell walker . . .').

At this point, ask for a face-to-face meeting. It's worth a shot. Some contacts may try to get you to settle for a phone call. Be honest: say that you learn much more by visiting people in the workplace. Say that you'd like to ask a short number of key questions. Ask for 11 minutes of the person's time. 'Five minutes' or '15 minutes' is too vague. You can conduct a REVEAL interview in 11 minutes, and if you stay longer it's usually because your interviewee wants to know more about you.

Face-to-face means you learn far more – about the person, the organisation, and its culture. It increases the chance of being remembered, and the chance of a long-term relationship. Face-to-face wins every time. However, if the person you need to speak to is a long journey away, make the most of online connecting, leading to a telephone or Skype conversation. If your contact is a long distance away ask, 'who do you know in my part of the country . . .?'

### It's a conversation

Now you've considered the benefits of information interviews and looked at the REVEAL script, reset your thinking by one notch. It's an interview, yes – because it has structure and purpose – but it shouldn't feel like one. Make it feel like a conversation. Don't make your contacts feel grilled; if they enjoy the interaction, that will encourage them to keep involved. Keep things relaxed, so it feels like an inquisitive and energetic exploration, a conversation between like-minded people rather than something stiff or transactional.

## Conducting a REVEAL interview

You've got there – a face-to-face meeting. What on earth do you say? The REVEAL method offers you a simple, effective script. Use the structure and suggested wording a few times until you get the hang of it and develop your own questions.

| REVEAL stages and key phrases | Notes |
|---|---|
| **R**ecap<br><br>*Key statement*:<br>'I'm here because . . .' | Recap how and why this meeting has come about. Remind the listener of who introduced you, and why the person in front of you has been recommended as a contact. Say what you hope to get out of the meeting.<br><br>Mention that at the end of the conversation you'd be interested in referrals (e.g. 'I'm trying to talk to about a dozen people in this sector'). At the end of the interview, you can then ask for further contacts. |
| **E**xplore<br><br>*Key statement*:<br>'I'm here to find out as much as I can about . . .' | Your opening question emphasises that you have asked for a meeting to help your exploration. So, get started. Perhaps open with 'how did you get into this line of work?' Move on to more in-depth questions about the sector you're exploring, e.g. 'What do you find most interesting about this sector?' Move the focus onto hiring patterns – how people normally get into this line of work. Probe the conventional and unconventional ways of getting work in this sector.<br><br>This part of the conversation is when you ask most questions. |
| **V**ision | You're asking your contact to improve your vision – so you have a clearer understanding of the sector you're investigating and how it's changing. A good supplementary question is: 'What changes can you see coming along in the next year or two?' |

| *Key question*: 'What have been the biggest changes in this sector recently?' | Answers will provide useful clues about additional research you might undertake, key players, and organisations you should be talking to. |
|---|---|
| **E**xcellence<br><br>*Key question*: 'What kind of people are doing well in this sector?' | Ask what top performers look like. This is far more effective than asking 'how do I get a job?' Answers will reveal the skills profile of successful candidates – useful information to store away for the first time you match yourself against a role competitively. |
| **A**ction<br><br>*Key question*: 'What should I do to find out more?' | By now you've learned a lot and you don't want to outstay your welcome. So, being business-like, you move to your next action: 'If you were in my shoes, where would you look next?'<br><br>Draw your interview to its conclusion by seeking ideas for organisations and sub-sectors to research. Make a note of suggestions. |
| **L**inks<br><br>*Key statement*: 'Thanks very much for your time today. As I mentioned, I'm keen to talk to a number of people in this sector. Who should I be talking to?' | Show how much you have valued the conversation. Build on the suggested actions by focusing on names of people – links in the chain of connections you're going to build.<br><br>Seek the names of two or three new contacts: '*Who else* should I be talking to? . . . Perhaps you can recommend a couple of other people who can give me an equally useful perspective?'<br><br>If no names are forthcoming, probe for:<br><br>• names of organisations<br>• names of information brokers, for example, branch chairs of professional bodies<br>• the names of helpful recruitment consultants specialising in this sector.<br><br>Make sure you get a *warm handover*: 'I hate ringing people cold. It would be great if you could phone ahead and let your colleague know why I'd like to have a conversation . . .' |

### Follow-up

Too often people think the best, natural follow-up to a REVEAL interview is to send a CV. Wrong – remember, it's a big ask. If you want to send a follow-up, try an email summarising your background, interests, and top skills in five or six bullet points.

However, the simplest way of following up is to send an old-school 'thank you' card. Yes, a hard copy one you send through the post. Write in it how the meeting was useful to you and what has happened as a result of it. This works, partly because many people only send thanks by email. A card says 'thank you' with more care and attention, and that's appreciated. Cards like this are hard to throw away, and often remain on a notice board or under the glass of someone's desk for several months. Ensure your contact details are included somewhere discreetly on the card so it's easy to get back to you.

Don't send further requests for help unless you really need to. It's much better if you send something helpful, such as a copy of an article, a link to a useful web page, a book recommendation, or an introduction to someone else.

### What if I am invited to consider a job?

Don't let the meeting become a job interview – that's a breach of trust. If a specific position enters the discussion, say you'd like to go away and prepare for a proper interview. Offer a time when you are free within the next few days. Ask for full details of the job and prepare thoroughly, even if you are in a shortlist of one. That way you come back fully prepared, matching your strengths to the key requirements of the job.

## Following the maze

It's easy to feel sceptical about information interviews. People naturally ask, 'how long does the process take?' and 'does it really work?' It's hard to predict in advance which conversation is going to get you the biggest result. It's like working your way through a maze. The treasure could be there at the first turn, around the next corner, or deep in the maze. You have to trust and keep searching.

The good news? Things happen along the way. You are likely to fall over vacancies. The jobs you find might not be right for you – pass them along to others in your network. You are also likely to have some fascinating conversations and meet some very interesting people. Thank them for whatever they provide, even if it's just encouragement.

## Three predictions

Here are three calculated predictions. The first is this. You already know at least one person who can really help you. When we begin networking, we scan the far horizon for contacts, people we know only vaguely. Who do you know who is close by? There's a simple test: you're looking for the kind of person you could pick up the phone and talk to without having to plan what you're going to say.

The second prediction is this. Whatever job search methods you use, you'll *probably find a job through someone you know already, or someone you meet in the next three months.* Play the game backwards. Who are you going to call for the first conversation?

The last prediction comes from careers expert Daniel Porot, who says that the best results come from the third circle of networking. The people you already know well are the first circle. They introduce you to second circle contacts, who you may already know vaguely. People in the second circle introduce you to an entirely new group – the third circle – composed of people you don't know at all. However, this third circle gives you the best feedback and the most useful leads. Why? Possibly because you meet people who make no assumptions about you. Not only that, but by the time you get to the rich territory of the third circle, you've got pretty good at the process.

## Exercise 15.1 – Who can you reach?

Networking for softies means that you start with people you already know, but it's useful to have some sense of where you want your conversations to take you. Start with the questions you want answered. What sectors do you want to know about? What organisations would you like to reach? What jobs do you want to find out more about? Start with a list of questions and topics.

Against each of these topics and questions, write a name. Someone who works in a relevant sector. Someone who used to work in that sector. Someone who knows people in a wide range of occupations. If you get lots of names that's great, but you only need two or three to start the process.

It's possible to build up a personal web of between 60 and 100 useful, curious, and interesting people within about three months. Keep a note of the name and contact number of people you are trying to reach. Have the list to hand in case someone calls you. Set a diary reminder of follow-up actions agreed.

# Exercise 15.2 –The Connections Game

As you investigate sectors and ask great questions, names of organisations will come up. Your personal research will add new names. Work towards a list of target organisations. You might eventually want to work for one of them, but at this stage you just want to find out more.

List them on a spreadsheet:

| Organisation name | Contact person | Tel/Email | Score | Next step |
|---|---|---|---|---|
| | | | | |
| | | | | |
| | | | | |
| | | | | |

Now play a game. In the 'Score' column give each organisation a score from 1 to 10. A score of 1 means you know nothing about the organisation apart from its name. A mid-range score means you know a lot about how the organisation operates, its style and culture, and the kind of roles they regularly fill. A score of 9 means you have at least two people inside the organisation, and 10 means you are close to at least one decision-maker capable of making you a job offer.

Use the 'Next step' column to record your planned follow-up activity. Every week, try to improve every score by at least one point. Reach out to people via LinkedIn or your personal network, and keep asking for warm introductions. This way you keep building connections until you're a known quantity.

# 'Must do' list: Ground rules for information interviews

- ✓ Use the REVEAL structure. Keep practising to build up your confidence.
- ✓ Don't stay too long unless it is at the other person's insistence. Don't ask to be shown round the building or site, but warmly accept the offer if it is made.
- ✓ Don't ask about specific job openings because that undermines everything you've said about the purpose of the meeting.
- ✓ How you operate reflects on the person making the introduction. Turn up on time, and don't ask for more than your contact can deliver.
- ✓ Be ready for the question 'and what about you?' Try out your two-breath message (see p. 218).
- ✓ Don't forget to ask for three names. It's very easy to go home missing one of the main reasons for the meeting.
- ✓ Get people to hand you on. Don't call cold unless you have to, and only do so when you're clear about what to say.
- ✓ Send a thank you card a week or so afterwards: it's an unexpected gesture, and you will be remembered.
- ✓ If you send a follow-up email, don't attach a CV, which is a conversation closer, but perhaps include three to five bullet points reminding someone what you're looking for.

# 16

# Getting better results at interview

'Take your life in your own hands, and what happens?
A terrible thing: no one to blame.'
**Erica Jong**

*This chapter helps you to:*

- Deal with interview anxiety
- Rethink interview preparation and performance
- Plan for tough questions
- Improve the way you get evidence across
- Negotiate a job offer.

For question-by-question preparation, turn to *Knockout Interview*. This chapter provides an overview of the worst of what an interview can put you through, and the best that you can draw out of yourself.

## How we only pretend to prepare for an interview

Most people take interviews seriously, but not interview preparation. People who interview for a living say they regularly see people who have not thought about the most basic questions in advance. Even in a competitive market, candidates think about questions but don't prepare answers. They expect the interviewer to do the work, dragging evidence out of them. Alternatively, they place great trust in their power to 'wing it' on the day.

It's a puzzle why smart people leave so much to chance; the most likely reason is that interviews induce stress, and planning requires us to imagine what will happen. We want to avoid thinking about the experience, so we don't plan for it.

### Interview nerves

Don't beat yourself up for experiencing interview nerves. For some people anxiety sharpens the mind, but others experience something like stage fright, with symptoms including trembling, a dry mouth, and forgetting what they planned to say. Although you can't conquer interview nerves overnight, the good news is that you can take immediate steps to reduce their impact.

For example, one symptom of nervousness is clumsiness – dropping papers, spilling your tea. Prepare for that by keeping just one piece of paper in your hand, refusing a drink, and practising sitting still. Another common symptom is a temporary inability to recall information. Your CV is packed with evidence, but somehow you can't think of what to say.

This is where preparation is most effective. First, have confidence in your power to anticipate. Exercise 16.1 shows you how to analyse job documents to anticipate questions. With only a small amount of practice you'll be able to predict about 80% of interview questions. Yes, four out of five. Most are big, obvious topics related to job content. You can no longer get away with saying, 'I've no idea what they'll ask me.'

## Exercise 16.1 – Shopping list

Find an advertised job vacancy that interests you. Obtain a job description. Take an A4 piece of paper and divide it into two vertical columns. Interrogating the job description, write out in the left-hand column the employer's shopping list, everything the recruiter is looking for.

List all the 'wanted' elements: qualifications, experience, know-how, etc. Work out what's essential, and what's desirable. Use your industry knowledge to work out all the stuff between the lines: the unstated assumptions.

Now put yourself into the interviewer's shoes. What would be top of your wish list?

On the right-hand side of your sheet, write in your matching claims and evidence. These should initially just be bullet points – you can develop detailed examples later. When you seek evidence, look again at the Skill clips exercise (p. 94) and the discussion about achievements (see Chapter 7).

## Match and shape

Interview time is expensive, and time is limited. Planning to improvise means you plan to experience stress. Good planning does not mean imagining the interview; it means matching evidence in advance. Look hard at what appear to be the most important aspects of the job (often the skills and areas of experience listed first in the job description). What would you ask about? What must be on the interviewer's checklist? Review your experience and find a piece of evidence to match each point. Now turn evidence into stories.

### Telling tales

Candidates often say too much at interview, frustrating the process and losing the interviewer's attention, so compress your evidence into mini-narratives. There are two main benefits. Your material becomes easier to remember, giving you confidence that good material is within easy reach. The second outcome is that you're more likely to keep someone's attention. We like stories, particularly if they are entertaining, attention-grabbing or just interesting. We remember stories for much longer than we retain information, and we remember energised stories even longer.

For every question topic, write down a rough answer based on something you've done (your story might begin: 'Let me give you an example of where I've done that . . .'). Edit this material so it becomes a story. A good story. A short story, with a clear beginning and ending. A story that sounds new and fresh (don't repeat phrases printed in your CV). Tell it as *your* story – interview clichés suggest you're just another nondescript candidate.

Practise getting stories across in about two minutes. You don't have to know the whole story by heart, but you do need to be secure on the words you use to introduce each narrative, and very clear about how you finish. Use a simple structure – for example, you might identify a problem, explain how you dealt with it, and talk about the final result.

Great stories add sparkle to your answers, drawing on the 'bottled' energy discussed in Chapter 4. Rehearse stories by saying them out loud at least three times. Half-prepared candidates say they have thought 'about' their answers. Fully prepared candidates know the *exact* opening words of their answers to tricky questions. Speak your lines in front of a mirror, checking that your body language tells the same story as your words.

### Working in the right room

Interviews can look like hard work. *Avoid doing any work at all in the interview room.* This doesn't mean being laid back (although being a little more relaxed always helps). The phrase is a prompt to remind you that if you work hard at anticipating questions and practising convincing stories, you've done all the work in advance. Do the work in your living room, not the interview room. Anticipate surface-level questions relating to the job description, and then dig deeper. Talk to people who know the organisation; find out how success is described. Now think: What's the worst question you could ask yourself, knowing your own gaps and weaknesses? Where do you need to sharpen up your evidence?

The human brain is troubled by the unfamiliar. Rehearsal and repetition trick your brain into believing you have done something so often it seems routine and easy. If your material is pre-processed, stories at your fingertips, you give more attention to what's going on during the interview. You listen to questions with more care, and – because your brain isn't thrashing around trying to come up with examples – you work harder on maintaining eye contact and building a relationship with your interviewer.

If time is really short, use a simple formula: **six plus three**. Match stories against the **six** items in the job description which you think are most important, and then get **three** additional points across about why you're well matched to the role. This is especially useful in initial, screening interviews, which are a quick check that you match essential criteria.

### First moments

You're being assessed from the moment you appear on the premises (reception staff are often asked for informal feedback about candidates). Dress one or two notches smarter than the normal dress code for the organisation. Leave your coat, bag and umbrella with reception – it helps to reinforce the feeling that you already work there.

As you enter the interview room, the opening moments are a kind of screen test. Content matters very little – it's all about whether you look and sound like someone who fits the role. Present yourself as an energised, relaxed person who's easy to work with. Speak clearly, audibly, and at moderate speed, even if you're just talking about the traffic. As you answer questions, everything you do should signal reassurance to the interviewer – you fit in, you can do the job, and hiring you won't look like an embarrassing decision.

## Exercise 16.2 – The Politician's Trick

Listen to a seasoned politician being interviewed on the radio. No matter what questions are asked, the minister always manages to make three or four strong points about government policy. The questions just provide an opportunity: the airtime is being used as a way of getting a particular message across.

You can use the same technique:

- Step 1: Look at the key areas of a job, and ask yourself: 'What three points is it vital that I make during this interview?'
- Step 2: Write them down, and rehearse a clear, concise way of talking about them.
- Step 3: Make sure you get those three points across at interview. Politicians know that their listeners can only hold a few ideas in mind at one time. Interviewers are much the same.

### Kate Howlett's Top 10 interview tips

Given that most people know they need to turn up on time, look reasonably smart, sound, and coherent, I've compiled my alternative 'Top 10' list:

1. Remember, you're the **guest not the host.** Allow the interviewer to play the role of host and enjoy the courtesy afforded to you as the guest. If you start to put the interviewer on the spot by saying,

for example, 'What's your management style?', they won't enjoy the interview so much. Often candidates have played the role of interviewer more than interviewee and find it hard not to undermine the interviewer. The host needs security of control over the situation and the accolade of being trusted to be the interviewer. The guest needs to be comfortable and looked after – understand this is not a weak position.

2. **People buy from feelings** not from cognitive thoughts. People feel more intensely if you offer pictures not facts. Pitch your achievements through well-told stories – involve and engage the listener, allow them to empathise.

3. **Integrity and enthusiasm are the hardest qualities for any interviewer to resist.** Integrity means that when working with you, they will always know what's going on and can always trust you. You won't undermine their own position or cause them embarrassment. Enthusiasm shows confidence, generates energy, and is infectious – they always love offering the role to the person who *really* wants it!

4. **Visualise a time you performed at your best** – play it in your head like a film reel repeatedly a few days before your interview to remind yourself of how brilliant you can be. Allow yourself to believe in your own propaganda. Then, at interview, perform from the part of you that performed so brilliantly in your 'film reel'.

5. **People watch for things to emulate** – observe and register aspects of other people's personality, performance, and appearance and decide which aspects feel right for you to take on board. Decide what the

'grown-up' version of yourself looks like, collecting ideas from colleagues to consciously create a more effective and powerful version of yourself.

6. **Perform from your work head not your home head**. Often people feel stripped of their title and brand when they lose their job. Be clear about your own brand – if you were an Operations Manager, you are still an Operations Manager and have the experience to prove it – your brand is your industry experience. If you go into an interview with your home head on, you are more likely to feel vulnerable, exposed, overwhelmed, and lack clarity of what you are offering. Go in with your work head – clear of your own brand and its appeal in the competitive marketplace.

7. **What are your weaknesses?'** There is usually something in a job specification you lack or where you lack experience. You could just ignore it at interview, but when the interviewer compares you with other candidates, this hole in your credentials is bound to be discussed. It's better to talk openly about the issue so you can put a positive spin on it and talk about how you plan to overcome this minor gap.

8. **It's not about giving a good performance but about giving the best performance**. You can pretty much guarantee that the company will have a good selection of strong candidates to interview with the requisite qualifications and experience, all of whom can pull off a decent interview. So, what's the point in being one of the crowd? It's not about taking part, it's about winning – there are no second prizes. Try to challenge yourself throughout the interview to consider not what's a good answer but

what's the *best* answer. Ask yourself, 'what can I say that nobody else can? How can I put it in a picture so that they *feel* more intensely, and I become a compelling candidate?'

9. **Determine three things you'd like them to think about you in the first 90 seconds**, and use all your powers of non-verbal communication to portray those three things. Plan it into your appearance, manner, gait, and tone. It's amazing that so often people pick up what you're thinking without having to say a word. In fact, only a tiny part of the impression you make comes down to what you say – everything else is non-verbal.

10. **Don't try to 'close'** – this sales technique gives people the creeps and they can see right through it, making you a less attractive candidate. People on the whole don't like to be sold to. Show how much you want the role, and give clear and confident evidence of your achievements with enthusiasm and integrity. Remember that in the final stages of selection, you will have at least one other candidate in competition – you have potentially a 50% chance of getting the offer. However well you felt you got on with the interviewer and however well you answered the questions, at this stage, you can guarantee your competition also felt the same! Keep up the job search right until you sign a contract.

**Kate Howlett, Managing Consultant,**
**John Lees Associates**

'At interview, be yourself, but the best half of yourself.' **John Courtis**

## Improving your performance

An interview is a performance, and every performance improves with practice. This isn't just about answering questions. It's important to practise walking into a room full of strangers and sitting so you look confident and calm. You need to practise talking about yourself. It's vital to rehearse stories so they are concise and energised.

How can you improve your skills as an interviewee? You might think the answer is to ask for feedback. Unfortunately, risk-averse HR departments avoid saying much more than a bland 'we enjoyed meeting you but found someone else whose skills and experience are a better match for the job'. You may sometimes get useful information if you asked where you could have improved your answers rather than why you didn't get the job.

The most reliable method of improving your interview technique is to find a safe space. Instead of relying on feedback from real interviews, ask for practice interviews with professionals who regularly hire staff. Ask to be interviewed using both your CV and a real job description. Instruct your interview coach to require you to use the exact words you would use in a live interview. Ask for objective feedback about what you failed to say, about body language, and about whether you say too much or too little.

### Preparing for off-the-shelf questions

Although interviewers sometimes come up with smart, new kinds of questions, most of the time what they ask is predictably job-focused, or 'textbook' and unoriginal. Here are some questions you are likely to hear most often:

**'Tell us about yourself.'** Sometimes, this is the opening question, and it's deceptively simple. An employer will want to press on with other questions, so will be frustrated if your answer lasts for more than a few minutes. Don't try to unpack your entire work history. Offer a quick overview of the shape of your career and summarise your key skills.

**'Why do you want this job?'** Employers like to hear career stories that make sense. Don't apologise for your CV or suggest that it's a series of random events. Rehearse a quick summary of your career that shows how it is a single story with different themes that knit together, and then talk about how the job on offer is the perfect next step for you.

**'Why are you changing career?'** Give a clear reason why you plan to move into a new sector. Don't dwell on what has dissatisfied you about past roles – discuss positive reasons for change.

**'What are you most proud of in your working life?'** Get used to talking about high points in your career, picking examples that show you are motivated and can add value in a role. Prepare stories of times you rescued a situation, delighted a customer, or handled a difficult project.

**'What motivates you?'** Be prepared to talk about what you have to offer rather than what you want to gain – talk about valuing the chance to use particular skills, opportunities to learn and grow, or to try out ideas. Stress the benefits to the organisation. Show rather than tell – don't just say you are committed, provide an example that proves you are.

**'Tell me about your strengths and weaknesses.'** This question comes up all the time. Plan to talk about three or four strengths required by the job – with good examples ready to hand. If there are any gaps in experience, emphasise that you're a fast learner. Don't linger on weaknesses or talk yourself down name one skill that you would like to develop further.

**'Are you a team player?'** Think about how work colleagues would describe your working relationships. How easily do you fit into a team? Provide a real example of what you've added to a team – or, even better, where you've encouraged a team to work more effectively. Don't give the impression that you prefer working entirely alone.

**'How quickly do you pick things up?'** Employers want a fairly quick return on the time and money they put into recruitment, so they love fast learners, people who can hit the deck running and can get up to speed with minimal supervision. Talk about a past job – or study experience – where you got on top of a difficult problem quickly, organised your own learning, and got results quicker than expected.

**'How do you respond to pressure?'** An employer wants to know what you will actually be like in a busy workplace, and how reliable and calm you will be when things start to go wrong. Give examples of times when you have met difficult deadlines or handled tricky people, kept your cool, and got the right result.

**'Where do you see yourself in five years' time?'** You don't need to name a specific role, and without knowing the organisation you may come across as naïve if you say, 'in your job!' Talk about what you want to learn and achieve in the new role.

See 'Safety zone responses' (p. 247) for more advice on answering tough questions.

### Show you're in charge of your career story

To attract a job offer, you need to convince an employer that you can do the job and you will fit in. You also need to show how *the job matches your career story.*

Think about the way you present your work history to date. Do you, like some candidates, apologise because your CV is 'all over the place' or 'a jumble sale'? As Chapter 11 argues, you have just one career, and there are advantages to talking about it as one, coherent, story. If you have changed jobs frequently, talk positively about reasons for change, and show what you learned at each stage. Rather than giving the impression that you've been moved around like a parcel, show how you took control. Even if something didn't work out, you can talk about what you learned from the experience. Talk positively about changes of sector. Interviewers respond well to phrases such as 'I guess I was lucky because . . .' or 'that turned out well . . .'. Look at every turning point in your history (see Exercise 4.2) and prepare explanations of where you made decisions and took control.

When applying for a new role, talk about what you will learn from it – and how it makes sense as the natural next chapter in your career story.

### Talking about competencies

Competency-based interviews require a special kind of preparation. Where competencies are listed in a job description, match them point-by-point in your application form or cover letter. Prepare for interview questions which ask for specific examples of times you demonstrated these competencies – for example, 'Tell us about a time when you had to motivate a team.'

Average candidates give generalised answers ('What I usually do is . . .'). Strong candidates talk about specific events. Look through your work achievements for good examples.

Set the scene briefly, outline the challenge you faced, talk about what you did, and what happened as a result. Competency stories will usually feature a mix of skills, underpinning knowledge, working style, and your attitude to work. If it's a panel interview and you sense that you will get one shot at the answer, make sure that what you say covers every part of the named competency. Even with highly structured answers, it's still a good idea to tell engaging stories.

### Safety zone responses

We've looked at how you can anticipate questions. Which questions would you rather avoid? What parts of your experience would you prefer not to discuss in depth? If there are questions likely to make you clam up, prepare answers which allow you to stay firmly in your safety zone. These carefully prepared answers are brief, upbeat, get you out of difficulty, and yet also communicate strengths.

Being brief prevents you getting bogged down in a difficult topic. Staying upbeat reinforces the idea that you can overcome difficulties and stay in charge of your career story (see above). A good safety zone response moves the attention from past to future. For example, if you were talking about being made redundant, you might say: 'Like a lot of people I was laid off when the organisation restructured, but it's given me a chance to focus on what I really want to do . . .'.

Work on these responses carefully before you go anywhere near a decision-maker. If you're dealing with an especially difficult topic (for example, you dropped out of university), have at least one second line of defence to anticipate probing questions.

### Interview Questions where safety zone responses help

**'Why didn't you complete the course?'** People drop out of learning programmes all the time, but it's often difficult to disguise the fact on a CV. Don't go into great detail about why a course didn't work for you. State simply that it wasn't giving you what you needed, and you made the decision to try something new.

**'What did you like and dislike about your last job?'** Likes – make a good match between the things that motivate you in work (for example, people, challenges, new learning) and the key things on offer in this new role. Dislikes – talk about things that frustrated your work performance such as bureaucracy or computer failure rather than talking about individuals.

**'How do you respond to criticism?'** Employers don't have time for ruffled feathers or workplace squabbles. Treat this question as if it is really asking about how you respond to feedback. Give examples of times when you have adjusted your working method or tried new approaches. Don't complain that the criticism was unjustified.

**'Why are you on the market right now?'** An employer wants to know whether you are moving on from choice or circumstances. If you were made redundant, mention this briefly, then talk about the work you want to do next. Avoid saying anything negative about a previous employer. If you've been unemployed for some time, emphasise your continuing learning and the range of organisations you have looked at. Don't complain about how difficult the market is, or how many rejections you've received. Employers will also probe for reasons for job change, so rehearse short, positive stories covering these issues.

**'How did you feel about working for someone so difficult?'** Avoid criticism of past bosses. Everyone's working style is different, so it's best to show how you don't let personality issues get in the way at work; give examples of where you have worked with a range of colleagues and bosses. Explain different strategies you have used to communicate with people you found difficult.

**'What's been the biggest challenge in your career?'** Prepare an example of something where you achieved success (or at least came out fighting). Negative information lingers in the mind of interviewers, so pick a positive story – ideally one that showcases skills that are useful to the hiring organisation.

**'We've seen a lot of talented people. Why should we hire *you?*'** You're unlikely to have one 'killer' feature that puts you ahead of the competition. Describe how your skills, know-how, and experience combine together in a unique way to make you the best person for the job. This is often a good opportunity to shake interviewer beliefs: 'You might assume that I don't have enough experience in this sector. In fact...'.

### Your chance to ask questions

As the interview closes, you get a chance to ask questions. When asked, 'Do you have any questions for us?', too many candidates politely say, 'No, you've covered everything in great detail, thank you.' Wrong answer! Interviewers remember the first and last things said at interview more clearly than anything else. Your final questions are a great opportunity to leave a lasting impression.

Some interview guides try to persuade you that an interview is an exchange, a conversation, and you should try to find out enough to discover whether you want the job. This is wrong-headed. An interview is about securing a job offer. You can decide whether you want the job by research outside the interview room.

Therefore, don't ask questions which introduce the idea that you have doubts. The purpose of your final questions is message reinforcement, not information gathering – you want to leave a final positive impression signalling your interest in the role. Prepare two or three great questions (ask only two – have one spare in case a topic is addressed earlier in the interview).

Before you ask a question, say something positive about the role. Then your question sounds like your buying signal: you like the job so much you want to know more. Don't waste the interviewer's time by requesting basic information you should have learned from the company website.

Two approaches will work. First, ask questions that show familiarity with key result areas. Clarify how results will be measured, and probe for more information about targets and outcomes you're expected to achieve in the first six months. Second, ask questions about the future of the job: What changes are anticipated? How will the job adapt to those changes? What learning opportunities are on offer? These questions not only demonstrate enthusiasm, but also help the interviewer imagine you actually doing the job. Once an interviewer has that picture in mind, it's hard to shake.

### Interviews with recruitment consultants

Recruitment consultants are professional selectors who make a living finding workers to fill vacancies for client employers (see Chapter 13). They don't make the final selection decision, but are critically important gatekeepers determining whether or not you get on to an interview short-list. Their credibility depends on presenting well-prepared, credible candidates, so if there's something about your dress code or interview behaviour that raises questions, an experienced consultant will probably give you feedback. Sometimes they will grill you about your suitability for a role – useful preparation. Additionally, because the recruiter has looked at the role in detail, you can ask for tips on matching your evidence.

### Rejection

In the average job search, you will be rejected more times than accepted. Even if you don't get the job, you can learn a huge amount about your perceived market value. It's trite to say that you shouldn't feel rejected if turned down by an employer. It may take a while to bounce back, and that's understandable. Do remember that candidates are rejected for all kinds of arbitrary reasons – sometimes simply because a large number of applications are received and only a few candidates can move to the next stage.

In any job search you will hear the word 'no' more often than you hear the word 'yes'. This is a neutral statistical fact that has nothing to do with you. Even the very best sales-people in the world work on the basis that they need to hear the word 'no' at least three times before they get a 'yes'. The problem is that when it is 'no' to you, it can knock you off balance. Be careful not to use it as evidence to support absolute statements: 'I knew I was unemployable . . .'.

### Talking money

You may be asked about what you want to earn at any stage in the process. The golden rule is that you keep off the topic until the employer wants to offer you the job – the moment when you have maximum leverage. If the topic comes up earlier, the danger is that you name a salary out of line with an employer's expectations (too low or too high).

If you're asked what you want to be paid, base your request on hard knowledge of market conditions. Aim at pay in the top end of the range payable for a role of this kind. Emphasise the value you can add and the size of the problems you will solve. Alternatively, saying 'I'm being interviewed for jobs paying around £xxx' is a good way of showing your market value.

In general, find out what money is on offer rather than naming your price. If the offer is too low, take some time to think about your next step. You might come back and ask for a better offer, or you might choose to renegotiate some other part of the job – see the checklist that follows.

## 'Must do' list: Questions to ask yourself before accepting a job offer

1. **Does this job add to my CV?** What will this job add to your career story? How will it help or hinder the way you present yourself to a recruiter in five years' time? Have you done this kind of job before? If so, what's new about it? What will you learn in this job? How long will you keep learning?

2. **What parts of the offer do I want to negotiate?** Work out what matters to you most from the long list of things that candidates regularly include in the deal at this stage – money, flexible working, leave, relocation or travel packages, start date, location, pension, health benefits, car, even job content. The important thing to realise is that you can only ask for leverage on a maximum of one or two points, otherwise it sounds as if you are being difficult. Second, never try to renegotiate something you have previously agreed, as this is seen as unprofessional and can cause the whole deal to collapse.

3. **What's the team like?** Don't just ask, find out for yourself. While the formalities of a written offer are being completed, ask to spend a couple of hours with the team you will be joining. This confirms your strong interest in the job, but also helps you to be sure that you will fit in, and tells you a great deal about organisational culture. If the organisation turns down your request, you might wonder what's in store.

4. **Do I understand why I am being hired?** If you're unsure what the role is all about, you should certainly

be seeking more information before acceptance. Clarity about what's expected of you and what problems you're expected to solve can help enormously with the first 90 days of the job. It's also useful to know what they see in you – the reasons you've been hired are closely linked to what the organisation will see as success (see below).

5. **Should I try to influence role content?** This can also be a good time to negotiate what you will actually be doing in the job. You certainly won't have the same leverage for at least another 18 months or so of taking the job, so if you feel there is any possibility that you can tweak the job description so that it suits you better, try including this as part of the 'deal'.

6. **What does success look like?** Get a handle on the way you will be judged within four months of starting the role. Ask about preferred outcomes and what's expected of you, so you don't face unpleasant surprises down the line.

# Looking for work after finishing study

'Of course, it is very important to be sober when you take an exam. Many worthwhile careers in the street-cleansing, fruit-picking and subway-guitar-playing industries have been founded on a lack of understanding of this simple fact.'

**Terry Pratchett,** *Moving Pictures*

*This chapter looks at ways of:*

- Using this book if you're leaving full-time education soon
- Building on your academic achievement
- Seeking work when you have little or no work experience
- Translating what you know and can do into employer language.

## Thinking through your options

When people finish one course, particularly at university, they often start another. Undertaking a year or more of **further study** may seem like the most comfortable option. It may lead to a qualification that will really assist in career progression, but it could be your way of postponing a difficult decision. If you're thinking about obtaining another qualification, you might like to ask: (a) is it an essential career requirement that will enhance my CV and attract a higher salary?; (b) will it be personally fulfilling?; and (c) am I just delaying the moment when I have to look for a job?

Choose your subjects for further study carefully. Avoid being press-ganged into a subject because someone else thinks it's a good idea or you're offered a place on a course. The qualification is more likely to assist your CV if it adds something important to your knowledge and skills, *and* it's a subject you find intrinsically interesting.

What other options are there? **Taking time out** may appeal. Again, the question is whether you want to delay your career start merely to indulge yourself, to put off a decision, or whether there are things you really want to do. There is probably no other time in your life when you will have such freedom to travel, but think about what you will learn from the experience. Employers need to see the relevance of your time out, and what you learned from the experience. Sometimes you can successfully combine travel with work.

For many people, this is the moment to begin **job hunting.** This might be your very first role, or the next job after a study break. You now have a choice: do you make the same mistakes all new market entrants make, or do you shorten your job search time by working smarter?

### Dipping your toes in the shark tank

If you've just finished studying, finding a job may seem a relatively undemanding task. After stretching your brain to think about quantum physics or linguistics, filling in online application forms and drafting a CV may seem brainless. This, of course, is why many of our smartest market entrants have weak CVs and unpractised interview skills: preparing well to look for a job seems so easy, they don't do it at all.

There are several questions to think about if you've just finished a course of study:

- Are you looking for any kind of job to start repaying your student loan, or are you trying to build the kind of CV you'll be able to talk about with confidence in ten years' time?
- What kinds of roles might you be equipped to do, both immediately and in the future?
- Where are the jobs? How do you set about looking for them?
- What are the channels to finding jobs? Is it all about advertised positions, job boards or networking?
- How do you apply the skills and knowledge you've learned in your studies? How do you talk about your qualifications in ways that employers find meaningful?

### Getting more out of times you have seen work happening

Think hard, now, about the information employers are most interested in seeing – evidence of working activity, and the skills you used. Look at times you have done any kind of work, or had even some small exposure to it: placements during an academic course, overseas work while travelling, paid work during term time, work experience while studying, holiday jobs, even workplace visits.

For any kind of work, paid or unpaid, dig into memory to remember what you learned, what you did, the contribution you made, and where you made a difference. Start to build up a detailed record, including job titles, company names, and details of specific projects. Aim to collect more evidence than you will actually need – so you can select the very best data for your CV, and so you have plenty of back-up material for probing interview questions.

# What to say if you have little or no work experience

When you are leaving full-time education, finding good-quality evidence for your CV can feel like a tough job. You may feel you don't have many skills, or you are not sure what an employer finds valuable. You may have a fairly good idea of your personal strengths and feel that these are the only things you can write about. You probably haven't yet really understood how to communicate your skills to an employer, and although you know that employers are interested in evidence of achievements, you don't feel you have many worth mentioning.

For all the reasons mentioned above, most school, college, and university leavers write an upside-down CV, where all the important messages are at the wrong end. You can read more about what goes wrong in my book *Knockout CV*, but the main point is that too many CVs major on recent academic success. These documents don't say anything about skills, know-how, and achievements until page 2, when a rather thin-looking work history is presented. Such a CV shouts out, 'I am a student who has had the occasional job', or 'I have little experience but some potential', rather than showing that you already have the skills to hit the deck running.

### 14 steps forward if you're new to work

Career Psychologist **Denise Taylor** provides tips for market entrants.

1. Build evidence of your employability while studying. School students don't undertake much part-time work, but you may have been babysitting or

volunteering and you will have evidence to explain your responsibility and commitment. Be clear about what you did, how it helped, and provide any details of things a bit out of the ordinary that stand out. Examples of times you thought on your feet and took action are great, but these examples don't have to be major – you are at the start of a working career that will last for 50+ years.

2.  Good evidence doesn't just come from work experience. Consider your extracurricular activity. Team working (through sport or an interest group) will demonstrate valued skills. As you write your first CV, be sure to explain what your role was in the chess society, tennis team, etc. Imagine that someone has no idea what you did – make it clear, because the detail will be helpful.

3.  Now is a good time to take on some voluntary work. This could be visiting a care home and talking to the residents, or helping with a campaign that interests you. This doesn't need to be a big commitment; just two to three hours a week over several months will provide a useful addition to your CV.

4.  Think about where your interests lie. Your first job is unlikely to be a job for life; you will have multiple jobs over your working life and some of the jobs you will do may not exist yet. Choose a first job that interests you and will help you to develop useful life and employability skills.

5.  Think about what you have to offer. You may have well developed technical skills, ability to code and understand about social media. These could be valuable to a small business and could be a useful part of a junior administration role. On the other hand, 'soft' skills such as the ability to persuade,

negotiate, or handle difficult customers will put you into roles which are less likely to be automated in the future.

6. Communication skills are important. Seek opportunities to get involved in discussions with others so you feel confident in speaking up and speaking clearly. This may mean spending a bit less time on your phone and more time talking to other people face-to-face – the more you do it, the easier it becomes.

7. Think about how you are going to choose your career. Find out what provision is available from your school, but don't rely on reading a computer-generated report. You may not know what jobs involve, so look at websites such as www.careers4u.tv where you can find out more. It also helps to talk to people who are doing the job, but beware, they may feel jaded, and realise they chose the wrong job!

8. Think about your experience and how you will make it relevant. When you see a job advert for a school leaver, or want to apply for an apprenticeship scheme, carefully read all the information provided and how you measure up. For a first job, an employer won't expect much experience, what they are looking for is 'potential' and whether you have a 'can do' attitude, so any examples of using your initiative should be included on your CV.

9. Describe your strengths, but be realistic about how far you 'sell' what you can do. Avoid empty claims, but also avoid undue modesty. Name your skills and say what happened when you used them, with concrete examples. If you find it hard to identify your skills, ask people you know to describe where they see your strengths.

10. Catalogue your accomplishments from different contexts: study, any work experience, hobbies and leisure time, voluntary activities. Try to present your achievements in interesting mini-narratives (see Chapter 16). Shopping is not an accomplishment in the eyes of an employer but is often included on young people's CVs!

11. Explain your qualifications. Employers are clear on A levels, but may not understand other qualifications, so explain what they included and involved.

12. Can you be clear about what motivates you? Think about when you are happiest. Is it when working on a problem, helping other people, being given a task to do? You may find it important to think about the likely values of organisations you will be talking to.

13. Get your message right. Work hard on your CV before you try to enter the job market. Look hard at the first 30 words of your CV to ensure they capture what you can offer an employer. Avoid flowery adjectives or claims you can't support (see Appendix 2 for a model CV and a range of tips). Few younger people create LinkedIn profiles, but using LinkedIn can be a great way to make connections and find a job.

14. Don't believe that interviews are a matter of luck. Prepare. Work out what the employer is really looking for, and work hard to communicate your matching abilities. Show employers that you really want to work in their field, not that they happen to be the first to have a vacancy.

**Denise Taylor, Career Psychologist with www.amazingpeople.co.uk and author of Find Work at 50+**

## 'I don't know what kind of work I want to do'

If you add up the thousands of hours students put into getting qualified, it's rather surprising how little attention they give to figuring out how they can apply their studies in work.

You may feel you are facing a bewildering range of choices regarding possible jobs and careers. Your problem may in fact be that you don't know enough about work to know which parts you are going to dislike. You may have little experience of work, or you may feel that your experience is not appropriate or useful to the new career you are hoping to begin.

Stuck for a career idea? Here are some first steps:

### Building career ideas

- Begin by looking at two parts of life for clues: what you enjoy doing (how do you spend your free time and what activities motivate you?), and what you enjoy thinking/talking/learning about. Look at what you love doing and try to find the opportunity to try it out on a work experience basis.
- Look at all the subjects that have interested you, and translate them into potential sectors of work using Chapter 10.
- Review your work experience. What has motivated you or excited you? Where have you been fully absorbed in your work?
- Look at the subjects you have just studied. What would you like to know more about? What skills have you developed while studying? Be very clear about your qualifications: why did you study them, what are they, what did they cover, and what are your grades? But when you apply for a job, list them after your skills and work experience, however limited that is.

- Take work experience and short-term work assignments seriously. Write down the skills you used and what you learned.
- Conduct an audit: What do you actually know about work? How can you find out more? Who can you talk to? Chapter 15 shows you how REVEAL interviews will help.

### Finding out

Don't miss out on obvious sources of information. If you have studied at university, you will have access to a university careers service. In a society where funding is largely being cut from careers services, the university sector maintains high standards of support and guidance. You will get more out of your service if you go to all the careers events on offer and, when you have a one-to-one session, if you have specific questions about areas of investigation.

Lecturers and subject specialists can sometimes help with industry contacts, but one of the best sources of help for graduates, even if you left university some years ago, is the wide range of alumni associations available. Few current students seem to make use of alumni associations, and it's worrying how many graduates don't draw on their services either.

The great thing about an alumni group is that members have signed up to help others in the same network. Sometimes there are ground rules about how much to ask, and how often, but the real strength of these groups is that members have effectively pre-contracted to help you. You don't have to say much about who you are or why you're asking – simply mentioning that you're a member of the group is usually enough. An efficient association should be able to put you in touch with former students. Talk to people who graduated in your subject two or three years ago, and others who have found work in sectors you find interesting. Send an email to establish contact, but see if you can get a face-to-face meeting, or at least a phone call. Ask members of your alumni association to be your first point of contact for information interviews (see Chapter 15).

Accept all ideas for career pathways gratefully, but make up your own mind based on evidence. Talk to anyone you can reach out to who is doing work which looks interesting. Where your studies are related to work, use them as a platform for your investigation. Most organisations will speak to you, for example, if you are carrying out a research programme, as long as your questions are not too extensive.

### Thinking rather than drifting

Many people in their forties and fifties say: 'I wish I'd thought more carefully about career choice when I was young.' Your first full-time job makes a big impact on your career.

Many people take 'fill-in' jobs after qualifying. If you start that way the danger is that you become a job hopper, snatching opportunities every time you feel dissatisfied, but never thinking about the overall shape and direction of your career. This experience can quickly lead to the idea that 'this is all there is' or 'this is what work is like'. You may convince yourself that the work you do will never be linked in any way to your studies. 'Fill-in' jobs can quickly become permanent posts unless you keep your goals in mind.

If you have little work experience, it's difficult to know what job satisfaction feels like. You don't get a sense of what motivates you until you've sampled work and experienced what 'fit' feels like. The advantage of traditional graduate programmes was that they allowed entrants to experience different parts of a business before choosing to specialise. The number of schemes has decreased significantly, but you can still adopt the career strategy of trying to replicate for yourself the opportunities provided by a good graduate scheme. Look for variety and range, particularly where you undertake unpaid work experience.

## Make a smarter offer to employers

Employers are often asked what skills and qualities they consider vital for workers competing in the twenty-first-century labour market. Owning your transferable skills means applying *and* communicating them (see 'Translation', below). Often the focus is on self-awareness – being able to identify your own skills, values, interests, and strengths, seek feedback from others, and seek opportunities for personal growth. Other job profiles look for assertiveness and the ability to identify, create, investigate and seize opportunities, goal-setting, organising your time effectively, and project management skills. Finding opportunities is one thing – the next step is to match them with your core skills and knowledge. Graduate recruiters often look for the ability to sell or negotiate. In a rapidly changing world, employers are often looking for workers who are flexible and capable of adapting goals in the light of changing circumstances.

You could also think about the career survival skills you will need. Networking is important as a source of advice and information, as Chapter 13 demonstrates. Political awareness can also assist in the long term – being aware of hidden tensions and power struggles within organisations (sometimes defined as spotting the person most likely to stab you in the back).

### Translation

The single biggest problem with CVs of university or college leavers is a failure to translate qualities, know-how, and experience into terms that are meaningful to an employer. This isn't just a problem for people leaving full-time education; people leaving teaching, the health service or the armed forces face the same problem.

Get in the habit of 'bridge thinking'. Busy recruiters don't have time to make connections unless they're obvious. It's your job to form a bridge between your experience and the world of the hiring company. Get an employer to see not just skills, but *transferable* skills – and they only become transferable when you communicate them *in terms an employer will get excited about.* For example, if you mention that you wrote a 6000-word dissertation, you will get little response. However, if you talk about why the topic fascinated you, the problems of gathering data, interviewing people, keeping up with the latest developments in your subject area, and working under pressure to achieve the project by a fixed deadline, then your interviewer starts to get interested. You have started to talk the same language.

### Identifying achievements

Employers get tired of hearing empty claims about the abilities of candidates, but they get interested when you can provide hard evidence, especially if you've achieved something. This doesn't have to be earth-shattering like climbing Everest or winning an Olympic medal. Achievement evidence shows an employer that you like to get things done, and produce results which assist an organisation and add to your CV.

Your recent studies may provide useful material. Some academic subjects mean little to employers, so explain why the topics you studied are relevant to a modern workplace. Talk about what you most enjoyed in study, what it taught you in terms of life skills, what special projects you undertook. Even if you studied something fairly abstract, you will have gained considerable experience of researching, analysing, organising, interviewing, consulting, and presenting information concisely and coherently in speech and in writing.

Look at all of your experience for evidence of skills, learning quickly, and having the right attitude at work. Look at your activities outside study. Perhaps you organised complicated or exciting social events, competitions or sporting activities, or you may have been a member of a society or club. Think about the transferable skills that you acquired from these experiences, and make sure they are mentioned in your CV.

## Taking unpaid work to build CV evidence

If you find it difficult to get a paid role, you'll almost certainly be offered opportunities to work for nothing to help you reach the first rung of the career ladder. At one time such opportunities were confined to highly competitive fields such as fashion or media, but now most large organisations have structured volunteer programmes. About 70,000 internships are offered every year in the UK, many unpaid. What impact does volunteering have on your career prospects? Does it make you look like a go-getter or a doormat?

Let's look at the downside. Even though you're working for an organisation with great values and purposes, you may still be stuck in a back room stuffing envelopes all day. With senior appointments the risk is that organisations place less value on your contribution and advice because they haven't paid for it. If you don't manage the event carefully or move on quickly enough, you can easily find yourself under-challenged.

You may give yourself CV problems if you stay too long or take too many internships. Research what your sector considers to be a reasonable length of time for an internship, and how many unpaid roles you can take without it looking like you are unable to secure a paid role. Keep in mind that while you are working, it may be harder to find time for an active job search. If there really are no paid jobs in your sector, you might be better off gaining experience in another, related sector for a couple of years.

One pitfall in working for nothing is that employers may leave you unsupervised while you undertake only low-level tasks. The critical question is what volunteering will add to your skills and whether it will enhance your value to future employers. Better placements include supervision, feedback, and development. Volunteer workers often recognise that they have a 'foot in the door': if a paid post comes up you are a known quantity with a distinct advantage over external candidates.

All work is a deal, whether it's paid or unpaid. You may feel the deal is entirely one-sided as you're working for free, but it's still possible to seek a trade-off between your contribution and any non-financial benefits available. Spot them in advance and negotiate the ones that matter most to you. You could ask for feedback on your performance, a reference at the end of the assignment, and introductions to key people. Other spin-offs can include exposure to new contexts, learning and development, and useful CV evidence. In job interviews, don't say 'it was just voluntary work'. Good volunteering experiences can add significantly to your employability.

If you apply for a job and you're asked to work without pay for a period of time, don't be offended by the suggestion. Continue to show strong interest in the organisation. You might indicate that this mode of working isn't right for you at the moment, but you'd like to be considered for any paid roles that come up in the future.

## Returning to a career after a study break

Those who have taken a career break to take a full-time course need to plan carefully when trying to return to the workplace. Taking time out to study places a gap in your CV, and doesn't always communicate employability; for a start, you have to convince an employer that you really are motivated to return to paid employment. You need focused answers to three questions:

1. Why did you decide to give up work to take this qualification?
2. What did you get out of it?
3. What do you hope to do next as a direct result of your studies?

If you fail to give an adequate answer to question 1, a recruiter starts to worry that you make random decisions in your career, or that you might be in danger of becoming a lifelong student. Question 2 requires you to think about *translation*, but also requires you to talk with enthusiasm about what you enjoyed while studying (after all, if you didn't enjoy it, why did you do it?). The third question requires you to communicate a clear, straightforward data-burst about the way this recent experience adds to your CV and has helped to reshape your career path.

## 'Must do' list: 10 steps to being job-ready if you're leaving full-time education

1. Your education may be the biggest recent event, but employers are only interested in your studies if they demonstrate useful skills or a high level of commitment. Explain your qualifications by showing how they taught you skills and knowledge useful in your next role.
2. Don't fill your CV with clichés and adjectives that scream out 'no experience, but great potential'.
3. Match claims you make about your skills with evidence. Give solid examples.
4. Catalogue any kind of experience that is work-related, including placements and volunteering. Look hard at the skills you used and where you made a difference. Use temporary work as a way of gaining skills and relevant experience.
5. Don't oversell your experience, but do explain it. Describe what you brought to the role, not just what the job description required you to do.
6. Plan for job interviews, don't wing it. List the requirements of a job and practise talking about your matching strengths.
7. Find someone with hiring experience to give your CV a cold read and to give you a general, introductory job interview. Prepare for it as if it's the real thing.
8. Reach out to people early in your job search. Ask around for ideas, leads, advice on your marketability. Talk to anyone who can move you closer to job-related information or a decision-maker.

9. Don't rely on job boards and advertised vacancies to help you find a job. You're far more likely to land your first role or useful work experience through word of mouth.
10. Take advice from people who regularly make short-listing decisions, not random websites or the opinions of friends and family.

# Master Sheet

The **Master Sheet** allows you to see the key ingredients in your ideal career on one sheet of paper. You can download this Master Sheet from the free resources section of www. johnleescareers.com – simply register to gain access.

## Completing and using the Master Sheet

1. Transfer results from the exercises identified – see the relevant page numbers.
2. Make a copy before you write anything in the Target Sectors box.
3. On one copy, write down any ideas you can come up with for Target Sectors.
4. Show the other, incomplete, copy to trusted friends. Ask the question, 'what sectors should I be exploring?' Write down their suggestions.
5. Review your Master Sheet frequently (try keeping a copy on the fridge door). Every time you look at it you may see new ideas and connections.
6. Your goal is to come up with five target sectors to investigate, and then begin your enquiries. Pick up the phone and talk to someone who is easy to approach.

# MASTER SHEET

**My top 3 career hot buttons** (p. 78)

1
2
3

---

**3 important items from my Jigsaw Job** (p. 40)

---

**4 top skills** (see Chapter 7)

1
2
3
4

---

**Relevant achievements** (see Chapter 7)

---

**My 2 strongest work themes** (p. 69):

1
2

---

**My most important values** (see p. 117)

---

**Subjects that fascinate me**

(House of Knowledge, p. 101)

---

**Target sectors – 5 sectors I plan to investigate**

1
2
3
4
5

# CV and cover letter tips

## Designing a winning CV

There are many ways of setting out a CV. The thing to remember is that your CV will only receive a few seconds of someone's attention before they decide whether to read further. This means that it is the first page of your CV that does most of the work.

Look critically at the first 30–40 words in your CV. What do they say about you? What conclusions do you expect a reader will draw from those words? If you start with clichés such as 'reliable', 'hard-working' or 'highly motivated', you've already categorised yourself as being the same as nearly every other candidate.

Think about whether you need to begin your CV with a **profile.** In general, if you are happy to stay in the sector you're already in, and just want the next big job along, you may not need a profile but you can start with your most recent (or current) job. However, if you want to make a career change, you will probably need a profile to make sure the reader interprets your history in the right way. It says pretty much what you would say if you were in the room handing the document over.

This Appendix includes an example CV in the style recommended by *Knockout CV*.

# The first page of your CV

1. Think of the first page of your CV as a **one-page advertisement,** which should be strong enough to stand alone.
2. A reader will probably have made a decision about you before getting to the end of your first page. Make sure all *key information* is here.
3. Write a **profile** if you want to make a career change. Mention your expertise, your main skills, the highlights of your work experience, and the sectors you've worked in.
4. Don't use **empty adjectives.** Almost everyone is creative, dynamic, enthusiastic . . . . Link skills to specific examples.
5. Be careful how you **label** yourself in the profile. If you use a previous job title, that's what the market will offer you again.
6. Don't include anything that strikes a **negative** note, such as difficulties you had with a past employer, or a failed course.
7. Put your **contact details** at the top of page 1. Include an email address, and make sure it's appropriate ('pleasureaddict@slaphead.org.uk' or 'dad@smithfamily. net' do not convey a professional impression).
8. Use summary words such as 'qualified' or 'graduate' to establish academic credibility.
9. List **important qualifications** and **training** on page 1 – if you know an employer will be attracted by what they represents.
10. Adjust the order of your bullet points so those matching the requirements of the job come top.

## Other things to remember in a CV

1. A CV only has one function: to get you an interview. **Don't overcomplicate it.**
2. Make your CV immediately **interesting.** The first 30 words matter.
3. Keep it **concise.** It isn't your life story.
4. Your CV should make **claims** about who you are and what you can do, and then provide evidence to back up those claims.
5. **Translate** what you know and can do into terms that will appeal to a recruiter. Talk about solving problems, making a difference, etc.
6. Say something interesting about your **academic history.** Relate it to an employer's needs rather than regurgitating the syllabus; for example, if you led a seminar or gave a talk, write about your facilitation or presentation skills.
7. Express **achievements** in terms of awards, money, time or percentages.
8. If you recently qualified, make sure you include information on page 1 about your work skills.
9. Include something under 'interests' that is neither bland nor run of the mill. Include interests that make you appear a rounded person, and those that have some relevance to the job. Make sure you can talk enthusiastically about any interest you mention.
10. Take some time to make the layout attractive, with plenty of white space. Don't print text so small it's painful to read.

# Example CV

## Jo Hope

Location: Newtown | m: 07777 000000 | e: jhope@example.com
LI: uk.linkedin.com/jhope27

A graduate information management professional with B2B experience focused on the information security needs of the insurance sector and a track record of achievement in building customer relationships:

- First-line technical support to business users.
- Redesigned user manuals and online customer support materials.
- Introduced customer satisfaction measurement.

EMPLOYMENT HISTORY

**Information Security Manager** – Nov. 2017–Present
ZZ Technical Industry Group

Responsible for a team of five colleagues providing first-line customer response around data management and security.

- Improved customer satisfaction scores focused on my department's work by 38% in the year to April 2018.
- Designed intranet staff training pages on internet security.
- Rewrote staff training manual.
- Seconded on in-house data security project for BigChain Plc in Q3 of 2017.

**Assistant Information Manager** – Jan. 2016–Nov. 2017
ZZ Technical Industry Group

Appointed to work alongside Information Security Manager in a new department rolling out a range of new service products.

- Key input into product range launched March 2016.
- Commissioned web tools from outside providers.

- Recruited, trained, and coached new appointments, all retained as of 2017.

**Customer Service Manager –**                     2013–2016
New Bubble Design

Taken on to provide and manage a range of customer service functions including:

- Liaison with clients about design needs.
- Managing a team of freelance designers.
- Keeping projects on target and on budget.

**Trainee Designer** – AZ Holdings                     2011–2013

Secured initial position against extensive competition as a trainee in a prestigious major organisation offering B2B interior design and shop-fitting solutions.

- Extensive client visits and consultations.
- My design for BetterShops front of sale literature featured in *Print*.
- Offered senior position but chose to move into consultancy work.

QUALIFICATIONS
_____

**Fine Art, BA Hons,** Newtown University, 2.1, 2011

**Diploma in Marketing,** Newtown College, 2013

**A Levels,** Newtown Sixth Form College, History (A), English (B), Art (A)

INTERESTS/VOLUNTARY COMMITMENTS
_____

- Helped organise DesignFest fun run 2017, raising money for children's charities.
- Active member of community group teaching digital photography/Photoshop skills to retired groups.
- Wardrobe Manager, Green Room players, Newtown.

## Features of the example CV

- The opening is brief and uncluttered. Do not title your document 'Curriculum Vitae', which sounds old-fashioned.
- It begins with the most user-friendly version of the candidate's name.
- In line with up-to-date formats, the CV does not include a full postal address but does include an email address and LinkedIn URL.
- There is just one phone number provided.
- It uses the word 'graduate' in the first line and saves more details about qualifications for later in the document.
- The profile avoids flowery language, too many adjectives, and unsubstantiated claims. It shows what this candidate might be doing next and points to measurable achievements which will be set out later in the document.
- A short number of bullet points are used immediately after the profile to give early prominence to key areas of experience.
- Job titles are indicated in bold so that they stand out.
- It does not say 'I' or 'he' but adopts an abbreviated, punchy style aimed at assisting a reader to quickly get to relevant evidence.
- Bullet points are used throughout; most begin with a strong verb.
- A short summary of the organisation and role is provided, leading quickly into more evidence of skills and achievements.
- It does not repeat obvious or dull information about past jobs, but emphasises hard evidence of added value. It pitches a strong message in the first half-page.

## What you should *not* do with your CV

1. **Don't** put any information on page 1 unless it says something important that might get you an interview.
2. **Don't** begin with CV clichés or information which confuses the reader about the kind of job you're looking for.
3. **Don't** put yourself down, or try irony or humour. It rarely reads the way you want it to.
4. **Don't** list referees. Provide details separately if requested. Talk to your referees every time you think they will be approached, and say why the role appeals to you.
5. **Don't** use obscure abbreviations or jargon.
6. **Don't** include your age or your date of birth.
7. **Don't** disclose your salary. It's generally best to deal with this at interview or, if you have to, in a cover letter.
8. **Don't** provide huge amounts of detail about jobs you did more than ten years ago.
9. **Don't** send out poor photocopies. Print on good-quality paper if you are posting or delivering a copy.
10. **Don't** include your reasons for leaving jobs, but be prepared to discuss this at interview in a positive way.

## The essentials of a great cover letter

Again, see *Knockout CV* for detailed advice on letter construction and further examples, and see the example letter below.

- The only function of a cover letter is to get your CV read, and to get you a meeting. Make your letter **brief and focused.**
- **Research** – refer to the problems, opportunities, and headaches that your target company is facing. Work out the main requirements of the job, and provide matching evidence.
- Match the top five or six **strengths required by the role** against bullet points summarising key experiences or skills. This short burst of information is the main content of your cover letter.
- Avoid beginning each sentence and paragraph with **'I'**. Focus on the perspective of the reader.
- When you outline your evidence, word it differently from your CV; repetition of exact phrases bores the reader.
- Don't put anything in your letter that gives the reader an excuse to put it aside, for example, apologising for your lack of a particular requirement, or mentioning your age, or referring to negative aspects such as why you left your last job.
- Don't start 'Dear Sir' or 'Dear Madam'. Address it to a **named decision-maker, even if** your letter is **speculative** (to a company that isn't currently advertising a job).
- Follow employer instructions regarding the recruitment process carefully – mistakes at an early stage can easily get you excluded.

## Example cover letter

---

**Your name and address**

Correct name and job title of recipient

Date

Dear Mr/Mrs/Mrs—

**Job Title/ Reference**

Please accept my application for the above post. Your work in this area interests me because..........

My CV is enclosed. I'd like to draw your attention to the following key areas which match the job content:

- Point 1
- Point 2
- Point 3
- Point 4
- Point 5

This role appeals to me because ..........

I'd value an opportunity to discuss the my application in person.

Yours sincerely

(Your name as it appears on the top of your CV)

---

# People who have transformed their careers

The case studies set out below are from clients who have worked with John Lees Associates and built their career change around ideas contained in this book.

## Melissa Carr, Assistant Operations Manager, third sector

Melissa studied Archaeology and Classical Civilisation at Nottingham University. After leaving university she felt 'lost', not knowing what direction to take. She began a career within the ambulance service, which was not right for her but provided an early indication that she wanted a career where she could 'give something back and do some good'.

Melissa then moved from working in healthcare to child-care. After working in a school for children with learning disabilities, she felt she had found her niche. She writes: 'I loved going into school every day and working with the children. However I did not want to go back to university to study teaching and I wanted more responsibility than being a teaching assistant. When I couldn't settle and decide what to do I decided to travel and work abroad, moving to Australia for two years. In hindsight this was perhaps an attempt to escape the real world of work and finding my career! I do not regret my time spent away and I had some excellent work experiences, but when I returned to the UK I felt more lost career wise than ever!'

Melissa's JLA career coach asked for an outline of her dream job. Melissa writes: 'I just had to find it! I received guidance on creating a CV that would get me into an interview. I was encouraged to network rather than sit trawling through internet job sites. During this time I was temping as a waitress in a university, far removed from where I wanted to be! I felt demoralised when several job applications were rejected. I began to network in the university and through this I was given the details for the agency where I now work. I sent my CV, which I wrote using the advice in *Knockout CV*. Within a week I had an interview and within two weeks I was working as a support worker for children with autism. After two months I was promoted to management. I had found a job where I was giving something back, but it also gave me the responsibility that I had craved.'

Melissa adds: 'I believe that having a clear idea of what I wanted from a job came across to my employers. They could see how passionate I was about working with children with learning disabilities. I have since moved on to other exciting roles in the third sector, building on the confidence I gained from my first big career change.'

## Mary Wilson, musician and careers counsellor

Following a degree in Social Anthropology at Cambridge and an enduring curiosity in what makes people tick, work cultures, and how people behave in groups and individually, Mary was drawn to working in the advice/counselling sector and enjoyed developing her skills as a one-to-one adviser and group trainer in a number of different fields including the Citizens Advice Bureau, a national charity, higher education, and a psychology consultancy. Weaving through this time after hours and at weekends, she was also a musician performing in a band at clubs and festivals.

Taking a few years away from the job market, Mary brought up two children while continuing to perform in her band. The time came to think about a return to work and Mary spent a few months working through *How to Get a Job You Love,* having attended John Lees' career coach masterclass. While Mary was comfortable with the idea of networking and talking to people about what they do, she needed some time to focus internally on what really mattered to her and work out what she wanted to do next. 'I felt as if I was drowning in a sea of creative ideas and didn't know which direction to follow.'

'Working through all the exercises in the book gave me a space to think through my ideas and even encouraged me to have some more! The book does not force you to make decisions too early but allows for lots of blue-sky thinking before laying out all the exercises on a giant sheet of flipchart paper. It was during this final process that breakthrough occurred, and I realised that I didn't have to decide between psychology and music but could see the links between them and gradually a vision emerged. I would be able to pursue a portfolio flexible career that also fitted around the needs of my growing family.'

After using the **JLA Skills Cards** Mary commented: 'Although I have highly developed people skills, I am most inspired by taking a fusion of concepts/ideas/sounds into a forum where I am in command. I need to be out there being radiant, full of warmth and empathy with a box of delights at my finger-tips. The toolkit needs to be maintained from the inside (requires time alone) and is full of musical instruments, imagination, psychological concepts and tools and ideas.'

Seven years on from this process Mary enjoys a portfolio career, mixing family life, freelance career coaching, training, and regularly performing in her band – and she also devises and runs lively music groups for babies and toddlers. More recently, she has expanded her toolbox to include violin teaching and sound engineering. Mary adds: 'Each year I look back at that giant sheet of flip chart paper summarising my values, interests and skills and find they still have an enduring quality. While individual goals and outcomes might be differently tempered each year, understanding what really motivates, interests, and puts petrol in your engine is surprisingly similar today as it was seven years ago. HTGAJYL really kick-started this insight and I'm very grateful to have read it.'

## Will Beale, Head of Programme Operations, WWF-UK

Will studied Natural Sciences and Chemical Engineering before joining Unilever. He worked in research, manufacturing, and new product development, but after ten years had a strong impulse to find his ideal career path. Will began by feeling apprehensive, but threw himself positively into the process: 'I spent three months undertaking information interviews with about 40 people in my target fields. I learned a lot but uncertainty about the future meant it was also quite a tough time, especially for my family.'

Will applied for a wide range of jobs – business, NGOs, public sector. His dream was to work for an organisation focused on environmental sustainability and nature conservation. When a job at WWF (formerly the World Wide Fund for Nature) entered his sights, he felt he had found the perfect match: 'It seemed ideal but honestly I did not expect to get it. However, by this time my application, interview and negotiation skills were well practised, and I knew how to sell the positive about myself.'

At WWF, Will has moved from quality management to building excellence in conservation management. 'To the general public the WWF brand is strongly associated with wildlife protection,' Will explains, 'but to achieve this we focus strongly on the underlying issues – such as climate change and drivers of unsustainable consumption. Whilst this makes the messaging more complicated, at every opportunity we try to recognise these connections.'

Will adds: 'what I love most about my work is when I have the chance to work with a particular project in more detail – for example, helping a team or organisation to develop a great strategy, or evaluating the impact of a major programme and considering how it needs to change. Over the last 15 years at WWF I have been fortunate enough to work with different offices and a wide variety of programmes in many wonderful places.'

## James Voûte, Player Experience Manager, London

After studying English Language & Literature at university, James was drawn towards the publishing industry and built a 14-year career at a global academic publisher that culminated in a senior leadership position. Although he never took the role for granted, he wondered if he might have found a job for life. However, he left the company following an organisational restructure and, two months later, his father suddenly and unexpectedly passed away.

'My life was turned upside down,' James explains. 'As well as the emotional upheaval of losing someone so close to me,

I went from what I thought was a stable and secure job to having no idea what I wanted to do next.'

James took some time out to plan the next stage of his career and approached John Lees Associates for career coaching as part of an outplacement service. By working through some of the exercises in *How to Get a Job You Love,* James was able to better understand what motivated him professionally and learned how to use his transferable skills to find a new role.

'My biggest problem was a lack of confidence,' James remembers. 'Because I found myself with very little career direction and no recent experience in recruitment situations, I built up a lot of barriers and limiting beliefs in my head. John helped me challenge those assumptions and also to think about how to access the hidden job market.'

Through his personal and professional networks, James learned of a strategic marketing role in the games industry, at a company he'd always been keen to work for. 'As it turned out, the company had been looking to recruit for this position for quite some time and couldn't find the right person. Although I didn't have a background in the games business, I was able to demonstrate I had a lot of qualities that were transferable and present myself as a good match for the role.' He was offered the position and found he enjoyed the organisation's culture, building strong relationships with a new network of people, and growing his skill set in a different industry.

'Looking back at the situation, if you'd told me my next job after over a decade in book publishing would be a role called Player Experience Manager at a games company, I wouldn't have believed it,' says James. 'It taught me that it's very easy to get defined by a strict set of beliefs and those beliefs can often be restrictive. By letting go of those preconceptions, I was able to grow both personally and professionally, and turn the corner during a very tough period of my life.'

## Beth Grant, small business owner, West Sussex

When she first came to JLA, Beth had been unable to work for three years following an accident at work resulting in a long-term shoulder problem. Initially, she could see very few work options and was worried about the kind of reception she would get from employers as a job seeker with long-term health problems and a long period out of the labour market.

Starting with JLA, Beth was encouraged by the fact that the exercises she was offered were tailored to her particular circumstances: 'All of the exercises completed were incredibly thought-provoking and were excellent in really helping you to think about what it is you want from a job and from life. Even though some of these were testing, with the amazing support I was fortunate enough to have, the end results far outweigh the difficult soul-searching moments.'

Not only that, the work she did boosted her confidence: 'At all stages we celebrated the progress I had made, and it was refreshing to be reminded of how far I had come.' With her consultant's knowledge, advice, encouragement, and guidance Beth found herself in a position to start looking at retraining and returning to work with a clearer understanding of her skills and the messages she needs to communicate to employers.

Beth learned to place the focus on what she can do rather than on her limitations, and in 2011 moved into the first permanent role since her accident, working as practice administrator in a busy, thriving orthodontic practice. She described herself as fortunate to have found an employer who valued staff and customers equally, but also rewarded hard work. She enjoyed the opportunity to return to work after the birth of her first child.

Beth stated: 'My self-confidence and self-belief have rocketed and using techniques I have learnt through my journey I have confidence I will eventually find the right job for me at the right time. When I started career coaching I was struggling to even contemplate the thought of returning to some form of work and did not believe it would be possible to change this.'

More recently, Beth has started her own business making handmade sewn goods and running an online store. She adds: 'I feel thankful that my past experiences have allowed me to develop and have the confidence within myself (although there are frequent wobbles!) to take the bold step of selling goods I have made from scratch myself. I now have the freedom of working from home doing something I enjoy and having the flexibility to also be there for my family, along with the pride of knowing I've achieved something for myself, by myself!'

## Simon Ryan, insurance research analyst and former TV location scout

Following a 12-month sabbatical after the birth of his son, Simon felt that he had reached an important crossroads in his working life. Having graduated with a construction degree, he'd worked in numerous sectors including construction, health and safety, event management, and property finance. Simon decided to investigate other options based on his skill set and experience. After a couple of unsuccessful meetings with recruitment consultants, he realised that assistance from a specialist in career redirection would be beneficial. Simon writes: 'I remember our first meeting and John asking me a question: when you're driving home from this meeting, what do you want to have happened to make you feel that it was worthwhile?'

The answer presented itself as their discussions progressed, and they explored areas that interested Simon, and also importantly areas that hadn't in the past. They discovered that his interest in buildings and property could be transferred to the TV and film industry, particularly finding locations for filming. Simon decided that he would explore this idea further, and set about researching location management.

Simon continues: 'From the outside, the TV industry can be perceived as a closed shop that can't be entered unless you are in the know, but if you are determined enough, you can find a way in.' A chance conversation with a family member opened a door, and Simon started to make contact with various location managers. The process was challenging: 'I gathered a list of people working in the area and contacted everybody in turn, with the initial purpose of asking them about their work, and any tips they could offer going forward, using the information interviews technique recommended. I was pretty much cold calling which in itself was tough, but I persevered and it paid off.' Simon began to form relationships within the business, and after four months he got his first job as a location assistant on a production for the BBC. Since then he has moved back to an enjoyable role in financial services.

# Index